THE XODUS FILES
REG COX • RICK BROWN
LEAFWOOD

THE X-ODUS FILES
Following God in an Alien Land
published by Leafwood Publishers

ISBN 0-9748441-8-7
Printed in the United States of America

Cover design by Rick Gibson

For information:
Leafwood Publishers, Siloam Springs, AR
1-877-634-6004 (toll free)

Visit our website: www.leafwoodpublishers.com

05 06 07 08 09 / 9 8 7 6 5 4 3 2 1

To our wives

Amy and Karen

for taking captive our wandering hearts

and pointing them towards home.

CONTENTS

These are the names of the sons of Israel who went to Egypt with Jacob, each with his family: Reuben, Simeon, Levi and Judah; Issachar, Zebulun and Benjamin; Dan and Naphtali; Gad and Asher. The descendants of Jacob numbered seventy in all; Joseph was already in Egypt.

Now Joseph and all his brothers and all that generation died, but the Israelites were fruitful and multiplied greatly and became exceedingly numerous, so that the land was filled with them.

Then a new king, who did not know about Joseph, came to power in Egypt. "Look," he said to his people, "the Israelites have become much too numerous for us. Come, we must deal shrewdly with them or they will become even more numerous and, if war breaks out, will join our enemies, fight against us and leave the country."

So they put slave masters over them to oppress them with forced labor, and they built Pithom and Rameses as store cities for Pharaoh. But the more they were oppressed, the more they multiplied and spread; so the Egyptians came to dread the Israelites and worked them ruthlessly. They made their lives bitter with hard labor in brick and mortar and with all kinds of work in the fields; in all their hard labor the Egyptians used them ruthlessly.

EXODUS 1:1-14

FILE 1

FROM WANDERERS TO WARRIORS

EXODUS 1:1-14

He has no address. But he does receive mail.

He has no phone. But he has a pharmacy that takes his calls.

He has no kitchen. But he has an array of restaurants that keep him well fed.

Mehran Karimi Nasseri is a wanderer. For sixteen years he has wandered in and around Terminal 1 of Charles de Gaulle Airport in Paris.[1]

Mehran was born in Iran but ended up living in limbo. At one point in his life he was imprisoned for demonstrating and expelled from his country without a passport. In 1981 he received refugee credentials but lost them when his briefcase was stolen in a Paris train station. In 1988 he turned up at the airport without a passport hoping to get on a flight to Britain. The officials stopped him but had no country to which they could deport him.

Sixteen years later he is still in the airport.

If the story sounds familiar, perhaps you've seen *The Terminal*, Steven Spielberg's movie about a man who lives one year in an airport terminal. Spielberg bought the rights to Mehran's story. It's the story of a man without a country who has learned how to cope in a place he doesn't belong. As Mehran says, "Here, it's not life. It's just staying like a passenger and waiting for departure."

EGYPTIAN WANDERING

When it comes to wandering and being displaced, Mehran has nothing on the ancient Hebrew people we read about in the book of Exodus. They too had longed for a homeland. Not for sixteen years but for over six hundred.[2]

The story of their wandering began when the father of Israel, Abraham, obeyed God's call and left his homeland in Genesis 12. Abraham is usually touted as the "father of faith," but he's also the spiritual predecessor of every man or woman who would look up from the security of their life as it is today and follow the promise of God into the risk of the unknown.

Two hundred years after Abraham's call his descendants wandered into Egypt and slavery for the next four hundred years. At first they were welcomed into this cosmopolitan giant of the ancient world. But soon political changes and a national identity crisis swept the welcome mat right out from under their feet.

Around 1720 BC many foreigners moved into Egypt from the surrounding nations who were facing various kinds of troubles.[3] These Semitic exiles made themselves right at home in this geopolitical oasis of the 17th century BC, settling in the north part of the nation in a place called Goshen. Goshen was fertile, safe, and serene. It was also the place the Hebrews would later occupy.

Meanwhile these non-Egyptian foreigners who had moved into the nation took on the identity of the Egyptians. After a successful revolt they took control of the country for 150 years. You might imagine how the native Egyptians felt about the takeover. It's like New Yorkers moving to Texas and calling themselves Texans. They didn't fight at the Alamo. They haven't owned a horse. Come to think of it, neither have most Texans. But you get the point. These foreigners took the name and the control of the land for one hundred fifty years.

Ownership of the land was seen as a divine right to native born sons and daughters of pure bloodlines. It was one thing to tolerate non-Egyptians living among them. It was another thing to be insulted by them and watch them assume the throne of control by force. The revolt fomented a rage the nation didn't get over until after the invasion of Alexander the Great 1500 years later.[4]

Somewhere around 1600 BC Joseph and the seventy descendants of Jacob arrived in Egypt. They accepted Pharaoh's invitation to come live in his land and settled in Goshen. But make no mistake about it; they wandered to Egypt because it fit the plan and purpose of God for their lives.

In 1550 BC Ahmose I, a true-blooded Egyptian, led an effort to remove the control over the land by the non-pure blooded Egyptians through a revolution.[5] His efforts succeeded. He overthrew the established government and reestablished a true Egyptian government in the land.

Egyptians had always disliked their neighbors living with them, but now they utterly detested foreigners. Ahmose expelled, executed, or enslaved all those who survived the bloody revolution.

Then, in an effort to establish a powerful military presence, Ahmose moved the capital to Memphis where the Hebrew people—our faith ancestors—were living. The move triggered dramatic building projects of temples and monuments made conveniently possible through the use of slave labor.[6]

Life in the capital was "not life" for the enslaved foreigners who were called *habiru*. Many believe *habiru* is the word Hebrew is derived from. It means "people without a homeland." It was hurled at the people of God as an insult, an emotionally wounding put down meant to say, "You're just a nobody! Nothing but a bunch of worthless homeless moochers!"

Habiru means *wanderer*.

WANDERING ABOUT—YOUR ANCESTORS

Do you see what this *Cliff's Notes* history review means? *Our faith forefathers were wanderers.* You and I come from people like Mehran who are living in transit. Blame it on God. He began the wandering when he decided to speak to Abraham. In Genesis 12:1-4 he says:

> *Leave your country, your people and your father's household and go to the land I will show you. I will make you into a great nation and I will bless you; I will make your name great, and you will be a blessing. I will bless those who bless you, and whoever*

curses you I will curse; and all peoples on earth will be blessed through you. So Abram left, as the LORD had told him.

Abraham left the comfort, the familiarity, the feel of the homeland he knew for no other reason than a promise. It was a promise of a foolproof future for his descendants. It was a promise that inspired them. It gave them their identity. The promise made them into a people defined not by geographic boundaries but by a promise. The promise of God.

And so Abraham picked up his bags and began wandering. Six hundred years later his ancestors were still wandering in Egypt. Six hundred years of airport living, waiting for a departure. Take a look at the scene in Exodus 1:1-14:

These are the names of the sons of Israel who went to Egypt with Jacob, each with his family: Reuben, Simeon, Levi and Judah; Issachar, Zebulun and Benjamin; Dan and Naphtali; Gad and Asher. The descendants of Jacob numbered seventy in all; Joseph was already in Egypt.

Now Joseph and all his brothers and all that generation died, but the Israelites were fruitful and multiplied greatly and became exceedingly numerous, so that the land was filled with them.

Then a new king, who did not know about Joseph, came to power in Egypt. "Look," he said to his people, "the Israelites have become much too numerous for us. Come, we must deal shrewdly with them or they will become even more numerous and, if war breaks out, will join our enemies, fight against us and leave the country."

So they put slave masters over them to oppress them with forced labor, and they built Pithom and Rameses as store cities for Pharaoh. But the more they were oppressed, the more they multiplied and spread; so the Egyptians came to dread the Israelites and worked them ruthlessly. They made their lives bitter with hard labor in brick and mortar and with all kinds of work in the fields; in all their hard labor the Egyptians used them ruthlessly.

These people were living as wanderers, aliens in a foreign land. Six hundred years of wandering. Four hundred of those years spent in slavery and backbreaking brickwork. But fast forward past the burning bush, past the plagues, past the Passover, the crossing of the Red Sea, past the wilderness, and past Mt. Sinai. Stop at Joshua 1:1.

> *After the death of Moses the servant of the LORD, the LORD said to Joshua son of Nun, Moses' aide: "Moses my servant is dead. Now then, you and all these people, get ready to cross the Jordan River into the land I am about to give to them—to the Israelites. I will give you every place where you set your foot, as I promised Moses. Your territory will extend from the desert to Lebanon, and from the great river, the Euphrates—all the Hittite country—to the Great Sea on the west. No one will be able to stand up against you all the days of your life. As I was with Moses, so I will be with you; I will never leave you nor forsake you.*
>
> *"Be strong and courageous, because you will lead these people to inherit the land I swore to their forefathers to give them. Be strong and very courageous. Be careful to obey all the law my servant Moses gave you; do not turn from it to the right or to the left, that you may be successful wherever you go. Do not let this Book of the Law depart from your mouth; meditate on it day and night, so that you may be careful to do everything written in it. Then you will be prosperous and successful. Have I not commanded you? Be strong and courageous. Do not be terrified; do not be discouraged, for the LORD your God will be with you wherever you go." (Joshua 1:1-9)*

Do you see what has happened? Between the crossing of the Red Sea and the crossing of the Jordan something has transpired. God has transformed the identity of his people. He has morphed them from slave *wanderers* to courageous *warriors*. He places some carefully designed steps in their way that take these ex-slaves from being a people who once could crank out bricks into a people who could wipe out seven nations at once.

God had a vision of his wanderers becoming warriors. People who were guided by his word.

God had a vision of his wanderers becoming warriors. People who would win battles. People who were not afraid of the sword.

God had a vision of his wanderers becoming warriors. People who were hungry for the fight. People who were fully confident that when they stepped on enemy soil it would become theirs.

Exodus is not about a people who got a break out of slavery. Exodus is about God preparing his people to have the heart of a courageous warrior. To have faith in him. To have a will to go to war and conquer lands in his name.

FROM WANDERER TO WARRIOR

Now, how in the world did God do that? How did he change a pack of house maids and boot kissing brick layers from wanderers into warriors? Well, he employed some interesting transformation strategies: four hundred years of slavery in the brick pits of Egypt. Forty years of the unknown of the wilderness.

Do those character crafting strategies sound loving to you? You see, those of us who have grown up accustomed to a comfortable form of Christianity have been conned into thinking conquering faith is formed through the touch of a velvet hand. We couldn't be more mistaken! There are a lot of bogus ideas of what kind of strategy God uses to change our character. Let us explain.

Some think God uses the *cosmopolitan strategy* to shape our character. This philosophy believes that God's goal is to prepare his people for social success. We're taught to believe it's all about you, so if you'll just trust God he will show you how to win friends and influence people. The cosmo plan of faith development aims to seek quick praise and crowd adoration (John 5:44). But this is a bankrupt philosophy that leaves us poor and empty.

Some say God uses the *affluence strategy* because he's preparing his people for financial success. Just send money to your local televangelist and God will open heaven's bank vault right into your checking account. This affluence plan aims us towards a self-serving security and "me first" goal. You will learn to notice the loss of stock but never the loss of food for the poor.

Then there's the *logic strategy*. This philosophy encourages us to believe that God wants to prepare his people for faith by ensuring that everything makes sense. If the facts aren't there, you don't follow. Logic trains us to walk by sight and not faith.

And finally, some believe he trains us with a *civilized strategy* so we can be comfortable. We are taught to reject invitations that require us to sacrifice. We are trained to want Jesus, but not his cross. We want to feel good about ourselves but seldom share Jesus in our neighborhood, work or community.

Why are these four strategies for character transformation wrong? Because their basic premise is that God is trying to enable us to become civilized...comfortable...safe and free from sacrifice. These are lies! These are counterfeit plans! Refuse these watered down visions of God's plan for shaping your heart! Following Jesus always involves a cross. Your destiny is not to become civilized. Your destiny is to become sanctified!

That's why bricks and wilderness don't make sense to you. But here's news for you: God's plan for you does not include the above strategies. Jesus died on the cross to train you to please God, not people. He wants to train you to have a heart for self-sacrifice, not for self-gluttony, to live a life of faith in the midst of your questions, to follow even when you can't see. Jesus did not die for our comfort. He died so that we would be equipped to comfort others.

GOD'S STRATEGY

How does the Army train its people? Does Boot Camp happen at a five-star resort like the Broadmoor in Colorado Springs? Are the recruits fed five-course meals three times a day? Are they given back massages and manicures? Of course not! Do you want people who have been trained in comfort and ease to go to war for you?

Neither does God. God wants to do with you now what he did with them then. He wants to turn you into a warrior. He prepares you through conflict and struggle, through wilderness times and wandering. But we may miss it. We miss that he has led us there to transform us. We are easily fooled into thinking that God prepares us with other strategies.

And so we wander.

We wander in our families. We go through the motions without any clear sense of what family is about.

We wander at our work. We clock in and clock out and mind our own business.

We wander at church. We show up on Sunday, act nice, and go home.

But we were not made to be wanderers. We were made to be warriors. We were born into a lineage of wanderers and outcasts so that we could become warriors. We were made for challenges. Why? So God could toughen us up and fill our hearts with the courage to face down the evil nations and see them fall.

You may be thinking: "What? Evil nations? Me, a warrior? You're getting a little carried away!" But listen to what God's word says:

> *Finally, be strong in the Lord and in his mighty power. Put on the full armor of God so that you can take your stand against the devil's schemes. For our struggle is not against flesh and blood, but against the rulers, against the authorities, against the powers of this dark world and against the spiritual forces of evil in the heavenly realms. (Ephesians 6:10-12)*

The word for "struggle" is a word that means "contest." It describes a fight where one opponent has thrown the other one down on the ground and has his hand on his throat. The apostle Paul is describing a hand to hand battle, one that is fought in the trenches.

We're then told to "put on the full armor of God" (Eph. 6:13). We need "full armor" because there's a battle going on that must be fought by spiritual hard-bodies, not soft couch potatoes. For example:

- 42% of the adult population believes having a sexual relationship with someone of the opposite sex to whom you are not married is morally acceptable.[7] There's a war going on.
- Christian marriages have as much of a chance for divorce as non-Christian homes.[8] There's a war going on.
- In the past thirteen years, the number of unchurched people in America has increased by ninety-two percent.[9] There's a war going on.
- Only 8% of adults said kids get better-than-adequate preparation in the spiritual realm, while more than 7-out-of-10 adults (71%) said children get inadequate spiritual training.[10] There's a war going on.
- The year 2003 "brought about increases in the proportions of people who contend that cohabitation (60%), adultery (42%), sexual relations between homosexuals (30%), abortion (45%), pornography (38%), the use of profanity (36%), and gambling (61%) are 'morally acceptable' behaviors."[11] There's a war going on.
- It seems that now the top influencers in American society are "the movies, television, the Internet, books, music, public policy and law, and family. The Christian church...is not among the top dozen influences these days...."[12] There's a war going on.

You were made to be a warrior.

You were made to train your family how to engage in the battle. You were made to change the texture of your workplace. You were made to be part of a church that equips you for the battle. When people look at your spirituality they should say, "Is that The Rock? Is that G.I. Jane? Is that Rambo? Is that Xena the Warrior Princess?"

God wants you to have the heart of a warrior. He desires to get you out of the holding pattern you've been stuck in. He wants you to leave terminal living.

If you want that too, then prepare yourself for a departure. Your flight is ready for take off. And it's time for you to board for the journey of your life.

Just grab your bags. We'll pack them as we go. All you need is time to sit back, adjust your seat, and read *The X-odus Files* with us at your leisure. Pay attention. Your flight is being called right now.

It's time to quit hanging around the airport.

It's time for your exodus.

...but the Israelites were fruitful and multiplied greatly and became exceedingly numerous, so that the land was filled with them.

EXODUS 1:7

FILE 2

A TIME FOR WAITING, A TIME FOR WARRING

EXODUS 1:6-2:1

It starts somewhere between the first and third helping of pumpkin pie at Thanksgiving. It grows as the decorations go up. It mushrooms as the tree is selected and the packages are wrapped. By now a monster has been created as the anticipation soars to the ceiling.

He's been waiting for this an entire year. As the time draws so close he can feel its cold breath down the microscopic hairs on his neck, the waiting becomes nearly unbearable. He begins by asking you, "Paleeeaaasssee. Just tell me what that present is! Please, please, please!" You do your best to help him put his mind on other things. "Don't you have some chores to do?"

But he is a persistent fella. Now he's on his knees. "Can I open just one? I can't wait until Christmas!" You hold firm. "No, you have to act like a big boy. You've waited this long. You can wait a few more days."

You discover how difficult this demand is. As you inspect the packages under the tree, you notice that taped edges have been pried open. "He's a rascal! He used his Swiss Army knife to make a clean cut!" Now it's time for a confrontation.

You corner him in the game room, his eyes fixated like a Zombie's on *Halo 2*. "Honey, you must stop trying to open all your packages. You're going to ruin the surprises the children have for you this Christmas!"

As hard as it is in our speed-obsessed society to believe, there is a time for waiting.

IN THE WAITING ROOM

Try telling that to the *habiru* living in Egypt. They had been wandering there for four hundred years. They had been waiting for just as long. They waited for the promise of God.

God had made the promise to Abraham six hundred years earlier. "I will make you into a great nation and I will bless you" (Genesis 12:2).

Later he threw in some real estate to sweeten the deal so the great nation would have a great place to live. "Lift up your eyes from where you are and look north and south, east and west. All the land that you see I will give to you and your offspring forever" (Genesis 13:14).

That was God's promise. And we promise you Abraham was not looking at Egypt when he was looking at land. He had just left Egypt in a hurry. Abe had some anxiety over the Egyptians killing him to get his wife Sarai, being the babe that she was. So he told them Sarai was his sister. That little lie was working for him until Pharaoh took her into his palace. Men taking women who aren't their wives doesn't set well with God, so he inflicted Pharaoh with serious diseases. When the Pharaoh found out Sarai was Abraham's wife and not his sister, he promptly sent her back to her rightful husband and sent Abraham packing (Genesis 12:10-20).

Egypt was fast becoming a distant speck in Abraham's rear view mirror. He was running away from Egypt to the Negev, which would become the southern part of Israel. At the start of Exodus his descendants are still in Egypt, not the land of the promise. And they're waiting. Not only that, they are doing backbreaking work. They are living in harsh times. It's not what they wanted but it's where they were.

Maybe that's where you are today. Waiting. Waiting in a place that isn't where you want to be. Maybe not even where God wants you to be. Is it possible that you can see your waiting as a time of preparation?

"How was the harsh labor of the Hebrews preparation? How can anything stressful that I've gone through be preparation for anything but heartache?" Good questions. One answer is that heartache can create a sense of urgency in us.

Urgency to change locales.

Urgency to change lifestyle.

Urgency to receive the promise.

Urgency to see God.

Joseph, the one who left his descendants in Egypt, left these deathbed words for his people hanging in the dry Egyptian air: "God will surely come to your aid and take you up out of this land to the land he promised on oath to Abraham, Isaac and Jacob" (Genesis 50:24).

Could it be that a time of waiting prepares you with an urgency to see God when he acts? You see your current reality and you decide it's not worth much. Too much busyness. Too little purpose. Hard on the back. Heavy on the heart.

And so an urgency surfaces in you for something more. You want God to come to your aid and take you to the land he has promised. But unprepared to see God we are often like the man caught on top of his house in a season of floods. He prayed for God to rescue him. In a short time a neighbor came by in a boat to pick him up. The man refused because God was going to save him. Then a helicopter spotted him and lowered a ladder for him to grab. He refused because God was going to save him. The man drowned and went to heaven where he asked God "Why didn't you save me?" God replied, "What did you expect? I sent you a boat and a helicopter. What else did you need?"

God is there, but we miss him. Waiting can build in us an urgency to seek after God so we will recognize him when he comes to our rescue.

Waiting also prepares you with a sense of urgency to get in on God's promises. Warriors want to get in on the action, feel the heat of the battle, and link up with what God is doing. But to paraphrase Jesus: the battlefields are plenty but the warriors are few.

When God's people are not engaged in the battle the following results occur:

- In one decade the unchurched population has grown from 24 to 34 percent.[1]
- Not one county in the entire U.S. has a higher percentage of churched people today than it had a decade ago.[2]
- 80% of the churches in the Western world are plateaued or declining.[3]
- 90% of kids active in high school youth groups do not go to church by the time they are sophomores in college. One-third of these will never return.[4]

Waiting can create in us an urgency for God to come. There is a time for waiting and it's a time for preparation.

HOW WARRIORS ARE FORGED

But waiting, compounded with the harshness of life, can make it tough to see God. Look for him in chapter one of Exodus. You read sixteen verses before you find his name. Then you only find his name two more times. Three times in twenty-two verses. It seems that Pharaoh and hard labor and killing baby boys get top billing. But make no mistake. God is there.

God is there and God is preparing. Look at verse 7: "...but the Israelites were fruitful and multiplied greatly and became exceedingly numerous, so that the land was filled with them" (Exodus 1:7). Remember the promise of God? The one where he told Abraham he'd make him into a great nation and give them the land of Canaan? The Hebrews aren't just making bricks in Egypt. They are being "fruitful" and "multiplying."

The language is insightful. "Fruitful" and "multiplied" are the same words used in Genesis 1:21, 22 and 28 in reference to creation. There in Genesis, God created something new out of chaos. And the same is happening here in Exodus. God is creating something new out of the chaos of life in Egypt. You don't see his name plastered all over billboards. But God knows what's going on in Egypt. And God has been working. He has been preparing a people the size of an army. Quietly, stealthily, before the Egyptians could do anything about it, the *habiru* had wandered themselves into a sizeable force.

That's not all God was up to. Even the struggle had a purpose. "They made their lives bitter with hard labor in brick and mortar and with all kinds of work in the fields; in all their hard labor the Egyptians used them ruthlessly" (Exodus 1:14).

Hard labor. Brick and mortar. Field work. Why? Pharaoh meant the harsh life to break the Hebrews. He thought the hard work would keep them from multiplying and keep them from teaming up with other nations for a mutiny (they would be too busy building pyramids to find partners).

But God took the harsh life and used it to build the Hebrews. They became more numerous. They became strong. Listen to how the Hebrew midwives explain their disobedience to Pharaoh's orders to kill newborn babies: "Hebrew women are not like Egyptian women; they are vigorous and give birth before the midwives arrive" (Exodus 1:19). God is building a strong people. A people who would not need to join up with any other nations to fight against Egypt. They would need only to join up with God.

It's both a physical and spiritual principle that you cannot become strong without struggle. Take for example the Lipizzaner horses.[5] The original stud for the Lipizzaner lived in the harsh Karst limestone at Lipizza in Slovenia. The Karst limestone causes hard hooves and strong bones to develop. This character trait was passed on only to the Lipizzaner. Its descendants thrive only in harsh conditions. These animals are slow to mature but they have a long life span. The Lipizzaners of Vienna are able to perform demanding exercises even when they are well over twenty years old. Some live to be over thirty when the average lifespan for a horse is twenty to twenty-five years.

Out of the harsh conditions prime stallions emerge. Out of the struggle of life warriors emerge.

Notice one more verse. "Now a man of the house of Levi married a Levite woman, and she became pregnant and gave birth to a son" (Exodus

2:1). While his people were waiting, God was sending a leader to the Hebrews. They needed someone who could show them the way out of their wandering.

The Hebrew people had been trained to follow orders from a leader. The Egyptian taskmasters got their way with them. When they said, "Jump!" the people jumped. The people did what they were trained to do.

But they were not doing what God intended for them to do. They were called to be a great nation. A nation to bless all nations. These wanderers needed a leader to show them the way. And because God knows what we need before we even ask, he prepares a leader for them.

He's done the same for you. He sent you a leader when he orchestrated another birth, the birth of his son Jesus. "And she gave birth to her firstborn, a son" (Luke 2:7).

God prepared a leader to come to our aid in our time of need. Paul put it this way: "God demonstrated his own love for us in this: while we were still sinners, Christ died for us" (Romans 5:8). Because God knows what we need before we ask, he worked while we waited.

Before we knew of our sin, God knew his plan for forgiveness.

Before we placed our trust in God, he placed his son on the cross.

Before we loved him, he loved us.

Before we gave our lives to him, he gave his life for us.

Before we served him, he served us.

And just as God sent a leader before the people knew they needed one, he sent Jesus to us before we knew we needed him. While we wait God works.

WHEN THE WAITING IS OVER

There is a time for waiting. It is a time for trusting. A time for building. It is a time when God shapes his people into an army ready for battle.

Maybe you sense that you have been in a place of waiting. How has God prepared you for the battle? You are the one God has placed in your family.

You are the one he has positioned at your school. You are the one God has put in your workplace. You are the one he has planted in your neighborhood. These places are enemy territory. Pharaoh has enslaved those around you. And you are the one God has chosen to carry out his desire to bless all nations, to *make disciples*.

Someone has got to sense the urgency of the times and quit building bricks. Someone has got to follow God into the taking of enemy territory. That someone is you. You are the highest leverage point in the places God has placed you. God intends you to be a powerful member of a sizeable army.

There is a time for waiting. But there is a time for warring. Warriors who wait too long get frustrated. If the waiting has made you frustrated then there's a good chance you have the heart of a warrior. Warriors who see the battle lines but are not engaged in the battle get frustrated. They are made to fight. And far too often when people who are meant to be warriors are not fighting the enemy they begin fighting each other.

Children—and some grown men—can hardly wait for Christmas. Warriors can hardly wait for battle. What are you waiting for?

Then Pharaoh's daughter went down to the Nile to bathe, and her attendants were walking along the river bank. She saw the basket among the reeds and sent her slave girl to get it. She opened it and saw the baby. He was crying, and she felt sorry for him. "This is one of the Hebrew babies," she said.

Then his sister asked Pharaoh's daughter, "Shall I go and get one of the Hebrew women to nurse the baby for you?"

"Yes, go," she answered. And the girl went and got the baby's mother. Pharaoh's daughter said to her, "Take this baby and nurse him for me, and I will pay you." So the woman took the baby and nursed him. When the child grew older, she took him to Pharaoh's daughter and he became her son. She named him Moses, saying, "I drew him out of the water."

EXODUS 2:5-10

FILE 3

I.D.ING WHO YOU ARE

EXODUS 2

"Swipe your finger please."

"What?" you say to the check out clerk.

"Swipe your finger please," she stoically repeats.

So, although you're not accustomed to doing so, you give her a finger—your index finger.

That's the scenario a company called Indivos hopes will become the norm. Indivos has developed software that scans fingerprints to process electronic payments. Frank Pierce, an Indivos spokesman, says, "You won't need cash or cards to pay for anything."

You can just hear their tagline now: "Your finger. You never leave home without it."[1]

Used for tagging criminals for more than a century already, fingerprints are now being utilized as keys to access buildings and computer networks, check out library books and buy food.

Fingerprints are reliable I.D.'s because there are no two alike. It seems to work too. During a three-year test at Visa's headquarters, more than 400 employees were involved in an experiment where 50,000 transactions were made. Not once did the system misidentify anyone. As a form of I.D., finger scans are expected to make up 33% of the market by the year 2006.

Your fingerprint I.D. may carry with it great purchasing power. Your life I.D. may carry with it a great influencing power. Let's scan Exodus 2 and see if you buy what we're saying.

GOD'S I.D. ON YOUR LIFE

We left the wanderers waiting in Egypt. And yet we've seen that they are becoming a great nation. How did they survive the harsh life of Egypt while other nations dropped off the map? They had God on their side. The people may not have seen God, but he has seen them. The people may not have heard God, but he has heard them.

> *The Israelites groaned in their slavery and cried out, and their cry for help because of their slavery went up to God. God heard their groaning and he remembered his covenant with Abraham, with Isaac and with Jacob. So God looked on the Israelites and was concerned about them. (Exodus 2:23-25)*

God sees and God hears. And God is concerned. He is concerned about what is happening to the Israelites and he is concerned about what is happening in your life.

So what does he do? He places his unmistakable imprint on us and gives us an I.D. An I.D. that is as unique as your fingerprint. He does it through individuals and disciplines.

INDIVIDUALS

God sends individuals into our lives to shape us. To wandering people he sends a leader. He sends a leader who can line the people up with God's purposes. Leaders play an irreplaceable role in how God shapes his people.

You have to admit, though, God sends leaders in unorthodox ways. No red carpets. No trumpet blasts. No Hollywood premiere. No, he sends a helpless baby to some unnamed parents and then has him hide for three months. Strange, don't you think? God's plans seem to rest on babies born in obscurity, whether in Egypt under an edict to annihilate him or in Bethlehem under an order to wipe out infants before they can walk. God wraps up his promises in unique packaging.

What he does with leaders he also does with his people. He places his inimitable imprint on your life. Could it be that before you were ever active for God he was active for you? Could it be that before you could ever speak a word God was purposefully speaking into your life, preparing you for his divine purpose? The psalmist put it this way:

> *I praise you because I am fearfully and*
> *wonderfully made;*
> *your works are wonderful,*
> *I know that full well.*
> *My frame was not hidden from you*
> *when I was made in the secret place.*
> *When I was woven together in the depths*
> *of the earth,*
> *your eyes saw my unformed body.*
> *All the days ordained for me*
> *were written in your book*
> *before one of them came to be. (Psalm 139:14-16)*

God shapes his leaders and through them he shapes us. And he shapes us as he shapes them. The journey of a helpless baby will show us how.

Although helpless, the baby had help. God placed individuals in his life that would shape him for life. You find the first in his parents.

We are not given their names. But we are given their character. The child's father was from the house of Levi and his mother was a Levite woman. The "house of Levi" will later become the priestly tribe, the tribe that is appointed to help people stay in relationship with God.

Has God placed parents in your life who have pointed you to God? Then be thankful. It is one way he is shaping you to be a warrior. But some of you may not have had parents who knew God. If so, has he placed some surrogate spiritual parents in your life? Others who have taught you and trained you in the ways of God? Then you too can be thankful. Sometimes God sends you spiritual parents to fill the void left by parents who may have cared for you but didn't know how to connect you with God.

This baby's mother was determined that her child would live and know God. For three months she hid him from the Egyptians. Imagine that! Ever tried to keep an infant baby quiet for three months? Think about the pressure she must have felt knowing that if he made one peep the Egyptians would be adding him to the tally of casualties from Pharaoh's edict. One Jewish story says that the Egyptians even developed a way to find these newborn Hebrews. They would walk past the Hebrew houses carrying an Egyptian infant with them. They would make the Egyptian baby cry hoping that any hidden Hebrew baby would cry too.[2]

The pressure became so intense the mother had to hide him in a basket and put him in the Nile. The basket is literally an "ark," the same word used in Genesis 6 and 7 for Noah's ark. That "basket" saved Noah. This one saves the baby. God places parents in our lives for a purpose.

At other times God places some unexpected individuals in our lives. Picture the scene: Mom leaves the baby in a mini-ark in the Nile. Sister is watching from a distance. Pharaoh's daughter comes to the river for a bath. Of all people, the enemy's daughter finds the baby. She sends for the mother and has her nurse him until he's old enough to come live with her. Then she does something significant. Don't miss it. She names him "Moses." Moses means "draw out."

This may come as a surprise to you, but God can use individuals who are not in his camp to shape you. It may have been a teacher. Maybe a neighbor. Perhaps an unbelieving relative. You saw something in their life that you learned from or were attracted to. Their sense of humor. Their positive outlook. Their concern for others. Their knowledge. Their skill.

Or perhaps they saw something in you. Better still they told you what they saw. "You're going to find a cure for that someday." "You can write songs that will encourage others when you're older."

Or they gave you a nickname. "The Rock." "Wild Thing." "Handsome One." (These are just a few that were given to us.)

The baby was called Moses. Every time he heard his name he was reminded of who he was and what he was to do. He was drawn out of the river. He was drawn out of slavery. He was drawn out of millions to draw them out too. He was drawn out by his mother's risky persistence, by her prayer for protection, by the princess's compassion. Most of all he was drawn out by God.

We have been too. God has drawn us out so he can use us. He uses individuals to shape us.

DISCIPLINES

He also uses disciplines.

Moses was raised in Pharaoh's house. There he would be taught about the Egyptian gods. There were gods for the sun, the Nile, war, crops, and the heavens. It took a lot of gods in the Egyptian world to run the world.

It seems bizarre. What is God doing placing his leader in a cultural mix where he will learn about other gods? He's preparing him to lead. The child is not alone. God is with him. And in this mix is his mother, teaching him about One God instead of many. A God who is Almighty. One who can run the universe by himself. Faith seeds are planted that will later bear tremendous fruit for God's people. His faith was shaped not in isolation from the world but in interaction with the world as his mother instilled in him a discipline of the study of God.

Moses would need other disciplines for his life. He got them as he was raised in Pharaoh's house to be a prince. "Moses was taught all the wisdom of the Egyptians, and he became mighty in both speech and action" (Acts 7:22).

History books tell us that Moses would have been taught reading and writing and hieroglyphics. It's not the three R's, but its close enough. He would learn how to copy text and how to write letters and other formal documents. Archery and horseback lessons got him outside the classroom. But back at his desk he would learn the languages of Canaan, the geography of Canaan and the script of Canaan.[3]

God let the pagan Egyptians equip his future leader with disciplines he would need. It made him familiar with the culture and the court of Pharaoh. He was readied to be one who would write down laws and lead a people to a land called Canaan.

I.D'ING WHO YOU ARE

Now it's time to put your finger on the scanner. It's time for you to take a break from building bricks and see how God has shaped you. Run your life over these three questions to reveal your unique print.

What leaders has God sent your way? Who over your lifetime has helped you line up with God's purposes for you? He wants you to follow them as they draw you out of your waiting and into his promises for you.

> *Remember your leaders, who spoke the word of God to you. Consider the outcome of their way of life and imitate their faith (Hebrews 13:7).*
>
> *Obey your leaders and submit to their authority. They keep watch over you as men who must give an account. Obey them so that their work will be a joy, not a burden, for that would be of no advantage to you (Hebrews 13:17).*

Submit means to get "under the mission." Godly leaders will get aligned with God's mission and help you do the same. Their job is to lead. Yours is to line up.

You may be thinking of leaders you have known in the past and leaders you know in the present who have nudged you closer to God. Some have been pastoral, making you feel safe and secure. Some may have been visionary, making you feel some tension between where you are and where God wants you to be.

How have you responded? We tend to be drawn to the pastoral but reject the visionary. But tell me, who do you want to lead you? The one who will leave you in a land that God did not intend you to stay in or the one who will draw you out—even when it means walking by faith?

Identify the leaders God has placed in your life. Make a list of what they have spoken into your life and see what God might be telling you. Then move to the next question.

What significant individuals has God placed in your life? Who, over the years, have you been drawn to? What about them attracted you? What words have they spoken to you that have shaped you?

An insight into the individuals who have influenced your life may be an insight into your I.D. We tend to be drawn to people who have character traits, skills, or behavior we want to emulate. God has shaped you through these individuals, showing you ways to live (and sometimes ways not to live). He has used some to connect you to him so that he can use you to connect even more people to him.

Don't stop there. Think through one more question. *What disciplines has he developed in you?* Paul advises us in Romans 12:3 to "think of yourself with sober judgment." In other words, know what you can do and what you cannot do.

Lance Armstrong took part in athletics at a young age. By the time he was 13 he was competing in triathlons. By 16 he turned pro. But he soon realized he loved cycling more than the running and swimming. So he decided to focus his energies on his favorite of the three. A number of years later Armstrong has become the first and only cyclist to win six consecutive titles of the Tour de France.[4]

Learn a lesson from Lance. You cannot do everything well. But you can do some things well. Can you sing? Give? Teach? Encourage? Write? Are you good with children? Play an instrument well? Build?

Whatever it is, you have been equipped with that skill so that God can use it for his purposes. You have abilities and interests that place you in enemy territory. God wants you there so you can make an impact on those around you. He wants you to take the land back from the enemy.

Discover your true I.D. and you may find you are set for success. You've been blessed with individuals who have nurtured you and disciplines that have shaped you. So why do you sometimes feel ineffective?

You need one thing more. You need a map. Moses had the best training in the world and he blew it. Thought he was ready to lead so he took matters into his own hands. Actually, he took an Egyptian in his own hands and killed him. Instead of leading his people, he took his I.D. and fled to the wilderness.

He was lost.

He needed a map.

And so do we. We'll look into that in the next chapter. Until then, be thankful that God has sent individuals and disciplines into your life.

They've helped make you into a one-of-a-kind person.

Just like your fingerprint.

There the angel of the LORD appeared to him in flames of fire from within a bush. Moses saw that though the bush was on fire it did not burn up. So Moses thought, "I will go over and see this strange sight—why the bush does not burn up."

When the LORD saw that he had gone over to look, God called to him from within the bush, "Moses! Moses!"

And Moses said, "Here I am."

"Do not come any closer," God said. "Take off your sandals, for the place where you are standing is holy ground." Then he said, "I am the God of your father, the God of Abraham, the God of Isaac and the God of Jacob." At this, Moses hid his face, because he was afraid to look at God.

EXODUS 3:2-6

"So now, go. I am sending you to Pharaoh to bring my people the Israelites out of Egypt."

But Moses said to God, "Who am I, that I should go to Pharaoh and bring the Israelites out of Egypt?"

And God said, "I will be with you."

EXODUS 3:10-12

But Moses said, "O LORD, please send someone else to do it."

EXODUS 4:13

FILE 4

FINDING GOD'S MAP FOR YOUR LIFE

EXODUS 3-4

Moses would become one of the greatest leaders of all time.

Multitudes planned their next step by watching his next move. Millions were driven by his directives. All the resources he needed lay within his reach. He was summoned for summit sessions with the ruler of the universe.

But before he got there he got stuck in mid-life. Maybe you've been there too. You don't have to be forty. You may be fifteen or fifty. You've taken stock of your life. You've inspected the list of individuals who have helped navigate your life. You've reviewed your disciplines: skills and abilities and talents.

The sum total of your I.D. possesses enough positives to project that you will have some impact in your world. Instead, your life can be described as "a lot of motion but very little movement." Your accomplishments are building but your life is breaking. And you're lost.

But you're not alone. Look closely and you'll see Moses. He was in a similar place. At forty Moses' career was going nowhere. The last entries on his resume were career killers: *Sand Burials* and *Flight Scheduling*. He was lost at mid-life, confused by his own questions.

Am I a prince or am I a slave?

Am I an Egyptian or am I a Hebrew?

Am I a believer in the gods of Egypt or am I a believer in Yahweh God of the Hebrews?

Am I a nation builder of Egypt's kingdom or am I a nation builder of God's kingdom?

He was a wonderer. And his wondering sent him wandering. Head in his hands, he ran from Egypt to escape. People do that when they are bewildered.

They run. Run away. Run to a bottle. Run to a lover. The running takes on myriad forms but the outcome is the same. The questions follow relentlessly until they are appeased.

Moses would become one of the greatest leaders of all times. He would eventually discover the answers to his questions. He would ultimately learn to lead courageously. But for now he is a wanderer. What helped him get on course with his life's destiny? A map. In the wilderness he found a map for his life.

MOSES AND THE MAP

But first he found a wife.

Moses fled to Midian and sat down by a well (see Exodus 2:15-22). While there, seven sisters came to water their father's flock. Some shepherds also came who ran the sisters off. Moses, being one who had zero tolerance for injustice, found himself rescuing the damsels in distress and watering their flock for them. As thanks for his effort, the father served him up a combo meal: food to eat and one of his daughters for a wife.

But he was still lost. So lost he named his son "I don't know where I belong" (Exodus 2:22). Maybe you haven't named any of your kids Gershom lately. But perhaps you have the same nagging question chasing you into the wilderness. A gnawing hunger inside keeping you spiritually unfulfilled. A scorching sensation that you have yet to accomplish your life purpose.

If so, don't run any longer. You're in a good place! Because it is the spiritually unfulfilled—those who have this recurring dream of something grander in life, something risky and adventurous—who are ready to encounter a burning bush.

Moses has become accustomed to tending sheep. From Pharaoh's grandeur to Jethro's pasture, Moses has swallowed a big gulp of humility. Day in and day out the same old rut. Moving sheep from one grazing field to the next. Wandering and wondering.

Until he spots a bush. A bush that is burning but not burning up. And out of this unusual burning bush comes the first piece of Moses' map.

MISSION

God gives Moses a mission. God identifies himself as the God of the wanderers. "Then he said, 'I am the God of your father, the God of Abraham, the God of Isaac and the God of Jacob'" (Exodus 3:6).

After forty years of questions, after forty years of wondering if he would ever live into his name, God tells Moses that he is not just a God for those who are born with a silver spoon in their mouths. He is the God of those who find themselves wandering in life. He is the God who takes wanderers and transforms them into warriors. He begins by giving them a mission. "I have come down to rescue them from the hand of the Egyptians and bring them up out of that land into a good and spacious land, a land flowing with milk and honey" (Exodus 3:8).

Mission gives life focus. In 1803 Meriwether Lewis had an encounter that changed the course of his life. Lewis was summoned by his Commander in Chief, Thomas Jefferson, and given this directive: "The object of your mission is to explore the Missouri river, and such principal stream of it, as, by its course and communication with the water of the Pacific Ocean may offer the most direct and practicable water communication across this continent, for the purposes of commerce."[1]

Of the many directions Lewis could turn in life, he now had one. He teamed up with William Clark and found himself charting a course to the Pacific Ocean and back. Two hundred years later we marvel at the feat. All because mission gave focus to their lives.

Mission did the same for Moses. Just as Lewis and Clark gained focus from Jefferson's mission, Moses gained focus from God's. The mission? Rescue God's people. For the warrior of God, mission answers the question: *What does God want done?*

The bush divides Moses' life into before and after. Before the bush Moses was about what Moses wanted done. He wanted the attention. He wanted to devise the plan. And he scaled the heights of ineffectiveness. After the bush Moses is about what God wanted done. Mission sharpened his focus: rescue and deliver God's people to a new land. The promise of God is wrapped up in the mission of his leader to rescue people. Mission gave focus to Moses' life.

It can do the same for you. Wanderers need a mission. God gives you one. The purpose of your life is inseparable from the rescue plan of God. He wants to send you on an adventure to rescue his people. But he doesn't send you empty handed. Look at the next piece of the map.

AUTHORITY

It's one thing to catch a glimpse of God's mission. It's another to be awakened to the possibility that he wants to use you.

God: "I'm going to rescue my people and give them the Promised Land."

Moses: "Great plan, God!"

God: "I am sending you to Pharaoh to bring my people the Israelites out of Egypt."

Moses: "Great plan.... *What?!*"

God's mission is the same for all. His assignments may differ. God assigns Moses a leadership position. Yours may be another. Whatever your assignment, God gives you the authority to do it. Authority answers the question: *What does God want "me" to do?* Don't discount your importance in the success of the mission.

God thinks highly enough of you to give you his authority to carry out his mission. Your understanding of this principle could be the difference between ineffectiveness and impact. It was for Frank Koch. Listen in on his naval experience.

Two battleships assigned to the training squadron had been at sea on maneuvers in heavy weather for several days. I was serving on the lead battleship and was on watch on the bridge as night fell. The visibility was poor with patchy fog, so the captain remained on the bridge keeping an eye on all activities.

Shortly after dark, the lookout on the wing of the bridge reported, "Light, bearing on the starboard bow."

"Is it steady or moving astern?" the captain called out.

Lookout replied, "Steady, captain," which meant we were on a dangerous collision course with that ship.

The captain then called to the signalman, "Signal that ship: We are on a collision course, advise you change course 20 degrees."

Back came a signal, "Advisable for you to change course 20 degrees."

The captain said, "Send, I'm a captain, change course 20 degrees."

"I'm a seaman second class," came the reply. "You had better change course 20 degrees."

By that time, the captain was furious. He spat out, "Send, I'm a battleship. Change course 20 degrees."

Back came the flashing light, "I'm a lighthouse."

We changed course.[2]

There would have been an impact of a different kind had the seaman second class not understood authority. He had been authorized to direct water traffic safely. He did his job regardless of what the captain thought.

Authority comes when the commander-in-chief gives it to you. Moses is told to lead. He is told to rescue God's people. Your assignment is similar. "Go, make disciples." And it is backed with authority. "All authority under heaven has been given to me, Jesus says. Therefore...go make disciples" (Matthew 28:18-19).

Good leaders will be on mission, with God, helping you carry out your assignment. But what if they aren't? What if you encounter leaders like the captain who are more focused on their rank than the rescue, more concerned with their own agendas than with fulfilling God's assignment? In that scenario you have to remember, as the seaman second class did, that you still have authority. You have a mission to complete that is clear and compelling: *Go, make disciples.* You don't need permission to carry out your orders. You don't need permission to teach someone. You don't need permission to go. It has already been given to you.

The One with all authority has included you in his position of power and told you he is sending you to rescue his people. All you need now is the final piece of the map.

PREPARATION

You need a time of preparation. Don't be surprised if the preparation for this mission is different from what you expect. At forty, Moses looked ready to assume leadership. And at forty he had learned well from the Egyptians how to lead. Arrogantly. Reactively. Forcefully. Independently. Moses tried to take matters in his own hands and came up empty. He wasn't prepared.

Hard to believe, isn't it? Above the surface he looked ready.

In his prime.

Schooled by the best.

Trained under the most powerful nation of the day.

But if he were to be a bridge over which the *habiru* would cross to escape Egypt and enter the Promised Land, he had to be solid below the surface.

Bridges need strong foundations below the water level. When the Brooklyn Bridge was built, the mission was clear: construct a bridge that would arch the East River and join Manhattan to Brooklyn. The Chief Engineer had the authority to build it. He also understood preparation. In June of 1872 he wrote:

> To such of the general public as might imagine that no work had been done on the New York tower, because they see no evidence of it above the water, I should simply remark that the amount of the masonry and concrete laid on that foundation during the past winter, *under water*, is equal in quantity to the entire masonry of the Brooklyn tower visible today above the water line."[3]

The Brooklyn Bridge is still serving citizens of New York today because 135 years ago someone understood preparation has to do with work nobody else sees. The same is true for God's warriors. Preparation answers the question: *What do I need to do it?*

Moses not only needed the "above water level" preparation of men but also the "below water level" preparation of God. He needed forty years of it. Only there would he find the power of God's presence he needed to serve God's mission with authority.

He needed solitude, so God put him in the wilderness.

He needed listening prayer, so God led him to the quiet.

He needed humility, so God let him hang out with sheep instead of in a palace.

Only then was he ready to lead. Before, he couldn't imagine God doing his work without him. Now, he's astonished God would want to use him at all. Moses offered up his excuses:

"I am a nobody" (Exodus 3:11).

"I don't have enough spiritual knowledge" (Exodus 3:13).

"I can't prove that truth is true" (Exodus 4:1).

"I can't communicate well" (Exodus 4:10).

"I just don't want to do it—get someone else" (Exodus 4:13).

It's exactly this mindset that is ready for God. This person is ready because now he knows that the mission will only be accomplished if God is in it. It's not about one's ability (although God will use one's ability). It's about a God who uses people who are available to him. God looks for those who have faith and he grows them into the job.

Moses asks the right questions. He asks, "Who am I?" Haven't you asked it too? God gives the command, "Go make disciples" and we counter with, "Who am *I*? I can't do it!" Moses' lack of confidence leads him to the headwaters of faith. It leads him to ask his second question: "Who are *you*?"

That's all any of us need ask. God gives the greatest answer of all time. Scholars suggest at least three meanings for the name of God given in this text: *I am who I am*. (I have always been.) *I am who I will be*. (I will show you who I am as I reveal myself to you.) *I am the one who causes things to be*. (I am the Creator of the Universe.)

Take your pick. The point is that Moses had to get his eyes off himself. Off his failure. Off his doubts. Off his wondering. Off the question *"who am I?"* and onto *"who is God?"*

Once he got the right question, he got his answer. *I am*. And with God's presence, Moses is prepared for his purpose in life.

THE JOURNEY BEGINS

Not bad for an 80-year-old shepherd who was convinced he'd missed his purpose and calling in life. He found himself before a burning bush and God, who instead of berating him beckoned him with love. A love that transformed him into a leader with a map.

And with map in hand Moses set out on a journey. It will be a journey from the ineffectiveness of his early life to one of impact that lasted beyond his life. People will be rescued. People will move towards a God-centered life. All because Moses had what he needed.

He had a mission. He had authority. He was prepared.

With the same map in your hand, you may find direction for your life. You may even find your way home to the heart of God.

Moses said to God, "Suppose I go to the Israelites and say to them, 'The God of your fathers has sent me to you,' and they ask me, 'What is his name?' Then what shall I tell them?"

God said to Moses, "I AM WHO I AM. This is what you are to say to the Israelites: 'I AM has sent me to you.'"

EXODUS 3:13-14

FILE 5

IT'S NOT ABOUT YOU!

EXODUS 3:1-15

On a TV "reality show" a woman who had a fear of heights was challenged to walk across a rope over a canyon gorge. She would have to maneuver herself across the rope several hundred feet above the canyon floor until she reached safety on the other side.

She was not left on her own. She had an instructor, a master skilled in climbing, who gave her instructions before she ever left *terra firma*. She knew the instructor's name, his credentials, and most of all she came to know his voice.

As she began her way across the ropes her fear set in. That voice inside kept saying, "You *can't* do this!" But there was another voice. The voice of the instructor. His voice kept telling her, "You *can* do it. Just take one step at a time."

The voice inside was winning out when she slipped and found herself dangling by her safety line. Head down. Staring at the empty space between herself and the bottom of the gorge. The instructor told her to start inching her way across while he went ahead of her to the other side to wait for her there.

Once he arrived on the other side, he kept sending her words of encouragement. She could not see him from her precarious perch. But she could hear him. And that was all that mattered. He got her across. Her faith in his words helped her conquer her fear.

TAKE THE "I" EXAM

Every day we are faced with similar fears. Not ones of maneuvering a canyon on a couple of ropes. But each day we maneuver through a gorge of voices in our minds that say, "I am not able to do it." *It* may be whatever someone in your past has told you that you could not do or that you were not good enough to do.

For us it happens weekly. "I'm not sure what to say on Sunday." "I'm not experienced enough to counsel this person." "I don't have a clue how to deal with this dilemma." The common denominator in these internal deliberations is the word "*I*."

We have been conditioned to look at ourselves first. We're not alone. Moses went through the same routine.

Moses had been tending sheep for forty years. It was a far cry from the hustle and bustle of Pharaoh's palace and his days in Egypt. His responsibilities have been focused on leading and caring for a flock of sheep.

Other than the bleating of sheep, the only other sound Moses hears is the slapping of his sandals against the sand under his feet. He is in the desert near Horeb. Horeb means "wasteland." The power and prestige of the palace have been replaced by the helplessness and humility of Horeb.

What do you think doing the same thing for forty years in a place called "wasteland" would do for your self-confidence? From the offices of Wall Street to pastoring in the pasture. Not much on which to build your resume or portfolio. But this has been his daily routine for forty years. Watching sheep. Directing sheep. Folding sheep. It is an ordinary, daily journey for him with no religious intentions. No expectations of a date with the divine.

But one day his routine is disrupted by fire. He turns to look and sees an ordinary bush that seems to be burning. Nothing totally unusual in a hot desert.[1] But as he does a double take Moses sees that the bush is not burning up. He sees no branches crumbling to the ground. He sees no ashes piling up below. This extraordinary sight is worth a closer look. So Moses moves with curiosity nearer the bush.

The sight of the bush burning is suddenly replaced by a sound. A voice calls him by name. You can imagine Moses anxiously glancing up, down, and around. He might have stared long and hard at the sheep. But he quickly realizes that the voice is coming from the fire in the bush.[2]

"I" TO "I" WITH GOD

Moses quickly responds with a noteworthy phrase. "Here *I* am." And thus begins an *"I"* to *"I"* conversation with God.

God says, "I am the God of your father, the God of Abraham, the God of Isaac and the God of Jacob. I have seen....I have heard....I have come down....I am sending you to Pharaoh" (Exodus 3:6-10).

Moses says, "Who am I, that I should go to Pharaoh?" (Exodus 3:11).

God says, "I will be with you" (Exodus 3:12).

Moses says, "Suppose I go and they ask me what your name is? What should I tell them?" (Exodus 3:13).

God says, "I am who I am. Tell them: I am has sent me to you" (Exodus 3:14).

Moses says, "I have never been eloquent. I am slow of speech and tongue" (Exodus 4:10).

God says, "I made your mouth and tongue. I will help you speak and teach you what to say" (Exodus 4:11-12).

Moses says, "Please send someone else" (Exodus 4:13). Translation: "I don't want to do it!"

God says, "I know Aaron can speak. I will help both of you speak and will teach you what to do" (Exodus 4:14-15).

Moses' ready "Here I am" turned into an unsteady "Who am I?" He has an "I" problem. He's focused on himself and not on God. And so comes the onslaught of canyon fears.

"I am a nobody" (3:11).

"I don't have enough spiritual knowledge" (3:13).

"I can't prove that truth is true" (4:1).

"I can't communicate well" (4:10).

Until Moses is finally just honest. "I don't want to do it" (4:13).

All the while God keeps instructing. "I am who I am." It's as if God is walking him across the canyon of doubt. He's saying, "It's not about you and who you are. It's about me and who *I* am."

Moses had it right. Who is he to go speak to Pharaoh and deliver Israel from bondage? That was a God-sized task. But God fully intended that he would be the one who did the work (Exodus 3:8ff).

But Moses can't see it because of his "I" problem. At least four times he repeats the word "I" before God replies with his emphatic "I am that I am."

Moses is seeing the wrong "I." And perhaps so are we.

BRINGING THE "I" INTO FOCUS

For instance, where do we tend to focus in this story? Some might say Moses. Others might want to draw applications from the burning bush. But the story has a voice, and that voice belongs to God. The sight of the bush and then the sound from within the bush are there to draw our attention to God's voice.

And it is that voice that declares its identity as "the One who always is." Present tense. God *is*, always.

In contrast to the great I AM is the succession of Pharaohs mentioned in Exodus. At the beginning of the book is the Pharaoh of Joseph's narrative. Next comes the king who did not know Joseph. At least one more is mentioned who replaced the king that died in Exodus 2:23.

The Israelites have seen many Pharaohs come and go. But there is only one constant God. And because he is, he is always with us.

So who is it we will focus on? Which "I" will get our attention? When you hear God calling you to a task, how will you respond?

You sense God tugging at you to see how you can help that young couple who seem to be having some difficulty. But you think, "I can't offer them any counsel. I don't have enough spiritual knowledge to do that."

But it's not about you. It's about God.

You pray for God to show you how he wants to use you. You love children. You hear that there is a need for a teacher. But you think, "I can't teach. I don't communicate well. I don't think I can do that."

But it's not about you. It's about God.

Your friend asks you about your faith. You know the Spirit is nudging you to share. But you think, "I can't prove what I believe is true. What if I mess things up? I'd better be quiet."

But it's not about you. It's about God.

How often do we remain immobilized because we look at ourselves first and list the resources we lack? How often do we want to say, "Send someone else!"? Listen carefully. That is the one response in the entire conversation that angers God. It angers God because it is a final denial that God can do what he says he will do.

But the burning issue we find coming from the bush is this: It is God who calls us and it is not about what we can or cannot do that is important.

It's not about us.

It's about God.

So take off your sandals. Listen up. God has something for you to do. You are on holy ground.

The LORD said to Moses, "When you return to Egypt, see that you perform before Pharaoh all the wonders I have given you the power to do. But I will harden his heart so that he will not let the people go."

EXODUS 4:21

Moses returned to the LORD and said, "O, Lord, why have you brought trouble upon this people? Is this why you sent me? Ever since I went to Pharaoh to speak in your name, he has brought trouble upon this people, and you have not rescued your people at all."

EXODUS 5:22-23

FILE 6

BUCKING THE SYSTEM

EXODUS 5-11

Hi. My name is Rick. And I am an addict.

Shocking? Oh, but so true. This week I admitted I have an addiction. Karen decided that we should eliminate caffeine from our lives. (I hear the gasps. Hang on. It gets worse.) One morning she substituted our full strength Maxwell House with a half-blend. (I know, I know. She should be locked away.) By mid-morning my head was pounding. By mid-afternoon I was unable to concentrate.

I had work to do that wasn't getting done. So I did what any resolute real man would do. I borrowed sixty cents from one of the kids at our church preschool and bought a Mountain Dew. Within minutes the highly caffeinated carbonate calmed my caffeine deficient cranium.

Able to think again, I pondered the predicament of the past day. How was this system of demand and supply created? Until thirty, I had never been a connoisseur of coffee. But until thirty I had never been double teamed.

You see, we had a new addition to our family. Our firstborn confused his days and nights. When most people were dreaming in bed he opted for bonding with his dad. He would wake up, bond and go back to bed, wake up, bond and go back to bed an average of four times a night.

I was a good dad at night but a grumpy husband in the morning. That's when he tagged his mother who then stepped into the ring. With her most tempting voice she whispered: "Try some coffee. It will help you get going in the morning." I was an unsuspecting victim, lured into the dark world of caffeine.

Soon after, God confronted me. "Did you drink of the coffee in the kitchen?"

I answered along with my ancestor Adam: "The woman you put here with me gave me some coffee to drink!"

Next thing I knew the system was in place. Wake up. Start the coffee. Drink the coffee. Sounds harmless. Until you try to change the system. A first attempt and I quickly realized that systems don't go away easily. They fight back.

First a dull pain. Followed by foggy thinking. Full blown headache. Pounding. The culture I had created was not going to go away without a fight. So I gave in and found another shot of caffeine.

What happens in our bodies happens in the world. Just attempt to change a system and you will find the system pushing back. Just ask Moses.

PURGING THE SYSTEM

Moses was up against a system that had nothing to do with caffeine but everything to do with captivity. For hundreds of years it had been in place: "They made their lives bitter with hard labor in brick and mortar and with all kinds of work in the fields; in all their hard labor the Egyptians used them ruthlessly" (Exodus 1:14).

The Israelites were enslaved by their culture.

Get up.

Make bricks.

Go to bed.

Repeat daily.

With every day the chains grew stronger. With every day the cries grew louder. God heard the cries. And he decided to break the cycle. So armed with God's mission, authority and preparation, Moses and Aaron embarked on a journey of obedience that led them straight into Pharaoh's court.

Applaud their nerve. Moses at 80. Aaron at 83. Stinky shepherds shuffling into Pharaoh's palace. Moses knows the corridors well. Each step reminds him of his childhood. Each step he relives the misery of his own people and the beliefs of the Egyptians. He saw the captivity of the Hebrews. He will later see that there were other captives.

Moses must have imagined a quick release. The two octogenarians go to Pharaoh and tell him: "This is what the LORD, the God of Israel, says: 'Let my people go, so that they may hold a festival to me in the desert'" (Exodus 5:1).

But instead of letting them go, Pharaoh let them work harder. He had supplied them with straw for the bricks. Now they would have to find their own. And, even with the extra workload, they were required to keep up the same quota of bricks.

The system will fight back.

The people took a beating under the scorching sun.

The foremen took a beating from the slave drivers.

And Moses took a beating from the foremen. "They [the Israelite foremen] found Moses and Aaron waiting to meet them, and they said, 'May the LORD look upon you and judge you! You have made us a stench to Pharaoh and his officials and have put a sword in their hand to kill us'" (Exodus 5:21).

Then God took a beating from Moses. "O, LORD, why have you brought trouble upon this people? Is this why you sent me? Ever since I went to Pharaoh to speak in your name, he has brought trouble upon this people, and you have not rescued your people at all" (Exodus 5:22-23).

The system will fight back.

You would think that God would have lost his patience with Moses. But he didn't. Instead he listened. Which is something Moses had not done. Earlier God had told him how things would play out. "The LORD said to Moses, 'When you return to Egypt, see that you perform before Pharaoh all the wonders I have given you the power to do. But I will harden his heart so that he will not let the people go'" (Exodus 4:21).

You're wondering, "How could Moses have missed it?" And we're wondering, "How do we miss it?" Jesus told us. "In this world you will have trouble" (John 16:33). "If they persecuted me, they will persecute you" (John 15:20). But somehow we expect to wage war with the world with a smile, a handshake, and a signed peace treaty. We expect powers to relent instead of resist. We believe that following God requires little struggle or sacrifice.

But we would do well to learn what Moses learned. The gods of this world don't give up their territory without a fight. Systems resist change.

God knew that. Moses needed to learn that. So God listened. He gave Moses again the words he needed to hear.

> *I am the* Lord. *I appeared to Abraham, to Isaac and to Jacob as God Almighty, but by my name the* Lord *I did not make myself known to them. I also established my covenant with them to give them the land of Canaan, where they lived as aliens. Moreover, I have heard the groaning of the Israelites, whom the Egyptians are enslaving, and I have remembered my covenant.*
>
> *Therefore, say to the Israelites: "I am the* Lord, *and I will bring you out from under the yoke of the Egyptians. I will free you from being slaves to them, and I will redeem you with an outstretched arm and with mighty acts of judgment. I will take you as my own people, and I will be your God. Then you will know that I am the* Lord *your God, who brought you out from under the yoke of the Egyptians. And I will bring you to the land I swore with uplifted hand to give to Abraham, to Isaac and to Jacob. I will give it to you as a possession. I am the* Lord. *(Exodus 6:2-8)*

Four times in seven verses. *I am the* Lord. God knew who he was. But Moses and his people didn't. They knew more about the gods of Egypt than their own. They had grown comfortable with the Egyptian belief system. It was a system that said its gods were powerful and should be catered to.

It was a system that was about to be changed. The LORD sent Moses and Aaron back to Pharaoh. The instructions? "Take your staff and throw it down before Pharaoh" (Exodus 7:9). Moses knew what would happen. He had practiced this before in chapter four. The staff would turn into a snake (Exodus 4:1-5).

Imagine his surprise when, in chapter seven, he throws down his staff and it becomes...a *snake!*

Perhaps you're scratching your head and asking, "What else would the staff turn into?" That's the problem with translation. In the Hebrew language, the first time Moses went through this routine the staff became a *nachash*—a serpent. This time the staff becomes a *tannin*—a monstrous snake, a reptile of horrendous proportions, a dragon or a dinosaur.

Pharaoh quickly calls security. His wise men and sorcerers come and "each one threw down his staff and it became a snake" (Exodus 7:12). Now enquiring minds want to know: "Were their snakes *nachash* snakes or *tannin* snakes?"

The small snakes (*nachash*) would tell us that the LORD is a much bigger God than their gods. We'd like that to be the point. Our battles will be against small enemies and over quickly. But the snakes in this passage are the large ones. The word is *tannin*. And the significance is that the gods of the world are big. They are strong and powerful. They are able to frighten us into obedience and hold us in their grasp.

Even so, the LORD can swallow them up. That's what happened in Pharaoh's palace. And it was a preview of what God would do to the gods of Egypt over the next ten rounds. One by one he took on all comers and one by one they were defeated.

- The Nile turned into blood.
- Houses became hostels for hoards of frogs.
- Dust in the wind became gnats in the sky.
- People were swarmed by flies.

- Cattle were dropping like flies.
- Boils landscaped flesh and hail pounded landscape.
- Locust devoured the leftovers.
- Darkness devoured the sun.
- Sons died at midnight.

Each plague pounded a god of the power system of the Egyptian world. God took them on one at a time. When the bell rang after the tenth round, Pharaoh let the people go. Moses emerged as the transformed leader of his people. But it didn't happen without a struggle.

COMPETING VOICES / GODS OF THIS WORLD

Your transformation won't happen without a struggle either. There are systems in your world more controlling than caffeine. Powers that you need to be free from. "gods" that enslave you.

Need some help seeing those "powers" and those "gods"? Some questions might help.

Why do you wear the clothes you wear?

How did you decide which car to drive?

What kids will you sit with at school? Which ones will you avoid?

Or try these:

How often have you shared your faith with someone else?

When was the last time you made time for a neighbor?

Would you ever do without something you have so those without could have something?

It doesn't take long before we find that those living in the land of the free are not as free as they think. Our cravings control us. Our eyes follow after things that please us. Our pride tells us what to have and do. Our schedules dictate how much time we have for others.

It's the world system (See 1 John 2:15-17). Culture tells us to do what feels good and we get addicted to pleasures. Money tells us to buy on credit and we get enslaved to debt. The world says those who have the most and live the largest are on top and we get shackled into filling our days with more work and more activities. All to appease the gods of this world.

Ever tried to change the world system? Sit with the kid at school who has been labeled an outsider and you will be treated like you have the plague. Refuse to buy on credit and watch the god of greed surface. Live on less and the powers that be will be less impressed.

The system will push back at you. When it does you will discover who your god is. When it does you will find yourself in a battle of tremendous proportions. The headache will come and coerce you into caving in.

Jake Plummer understands. He was pressured by the "god of conformity" in the National Football League. Jake found out how the system fights back when he applied a small #40 sticker to his helmet. "40" was the number his good friend Pat Tillman wore when they both played for the Arizona Cardinals. Tillman was killed in April 2004 while serving as an Army Ranger in Afghanistan.

Plummer wanted to pay a tribute to Tillman by wearing his number on his Denver Bronco helmet. A small gesture. But it bucked the system. Suddenly Jake the Snake found himself surrounded by the snakes of the NFL power machine. He was told he would be fined $30,000 if he continued to wear the sticker.

It would have been easy for him to step back. Instead, he stepped up. And soon others followed him in an outcry. Senator John McCain even got in on the act. He wrote the commissioner and said, "Pat Tillman left this world as a protector of our freedoms, the same freedoms that your league enjoys each Sunday. He died so that we as Americans can enjoy our way of life and express ourselves in the way that Jake Plummer now seeks to express himself."[1]

The system broke down. Jake got what he wanted. He gave up wearing the number, but he got a large #40 logo placed by the clock in the north end zone of Invesco Field at Mile High. The team runs ads on the scoreboard for the Pat Tillman Foundation. Plummer was asked to tape a public service announcement to honor his friend. And the NFL will donate $250,000 to a USO center in Afghanistan to be named after Tillman. Because Jake the Snake stood strong, Tillman is honored in a much bigger way.

And when we stand strong against the systems of this world, God is honored in a big way. Each time we step out in faith we give him the opportunity to show us who he will be. And each time he shows us we gain confidence that the one who said he would be with us is.

Moses entered the fray afraid to speak. God gave him Aaron as a mouthpiece. By the end of the plagues Moses does all the talking. His faith has grown. He has been seasoned by the battle.

You will be too. But you have to stand and fight. You have to understand that there is a battle going on. Name the systems that control your world. The gods that control you may be named anxiety, pride, envy, greed, lust, social forces or psychological forces. And with God's help go after them.

The result is that you will be freed. You will find that God has come to your rescue and led you to a way out.

What may surprise you is you won't go out alone. That's what Moses discovered. When he led the Israelites out of Egypt, Pharaoh was glad to see them go. They went with silver, gold, and droves of livestock.

But that's not all they left with. We're also told that "many *other people* went up with them" (Exodus 12:37). Most scholars believe the "other people" were Egyptians—people who had seen the power of God in the changed lives of his people. They saw a people who believed in the one God rather than the gods of the world.

And they followed. They followed because they saw others who had been enslaved by a world system become free.

Buck the systems of your world and see who follows you.

As Pharaoh approached, the Israelites looked up, and there were the Egyptians, marching after them. They were terrified and cried out to the LORD. They said to Moses, "Was it because there were no graves in Egypt that you brought us to the desert to die? What have you done to us by bringing us out of Egypt? Didn't we say to you in Egypt, 'Leave us alone; let us serve the Egyptians'? It would have been better for us to serve the Egyptians than to die in the desert!"

Moses answered the people, "Do not be afraid. Stand firm and you will see the deliverance the LORD will bring you today. The Egyptians you see today you will never see again. The LORD will fight for you; you need only to be still."

EXODUS 14:10-14

FILE 7

HOW FAITH CAN BEGIN WITH FEAR

EXODUS 13:17-15:21

You're *here*: a person prone to wandering. You want to be *there*: a seasoned warrior. The only thing stopping your move from one place to the other is a choice. You can either act out of fear or you can act out of faith.

Felix Baumgartner understands the choice. As base jumpers usually do, he found himself in an unusual place. Standing on the right hand of Jesus on the Christo Redentor statue in Rio de Janeiro.

Here's how he got there. He spent months training in his Salzburg home on a crane. Then he took his jumping equipment—including a crossbow—straight through Brazilian customs. He told them he was an archer traveling to a sports tournament.

Felix, known as "BASE 502" to his fans, hid overnight in the security area at—where else—the *base* of the statue. Just before dawn on Wednesday, December 1, 1999, "502" fired a cable from his crossbow over the right arm of the 98-foot statue. Then he climbed up the outstretched arm of the Christo Redentor.

He found himself in an unusual place: on the right hand of the Christ statue. He knew he wanted to perform a perfect jump and land on the ground below. But this would be the shortest base jump in history. Normally a base jumper needs fifty or sixty meters. This jump would be only thirty.[1]

His fears could have been numerous. Fear of heights. Fear of misjudgment. Fear of equipment failure. Fear of authorities below.

But he chose faith. Faith in his training. Faith in his calculations. Faith in the equipment. Faith in the escape plan.

So he jumped. He took a leap of faith and steered his parachute over shantytowns to a car park where his getaway car was waiting. The trip from here to there took only two and a half seconds.

"As I was standing on the hand, no more than 20 centimeters (8 inches) wide, looking into the rising sun I realized that I would never feel anything like this in my life again," Felix said in a statement.[2]

THE ESSENTIAL QUESTION

About a million Israelites could say the same. They had been in Egypt. They wanted to be in the Promised Land. They had been wanderers. God wanted them to be warriors. But they found themselves in an unusual place. Standing with a wall of water on one side and six elite Egyptian combat divisions on the other. They must have thought they would never feel anything like this again.

Perhaps you too could say the same. You find yourself in an unusual place. Trapped by your own fears. Standing on an unsteady twenty centimeters of self-doubt. Wanting to leave your own private slaveries but faced with a choice.

For those wanting to move from the "here" of *wandering* to the "there" of *warring*, the essential question is: Will you act out of fear or act out of faith? Your answer to that question holds the possibility of transforming your life.

It will make the difference between whether you live your life as a wanderer or a warrior.

It will make the difference between whether you live your life as a good church member curled up on a comfortable couch or a disciple who takes death defying leaps of faith into God's preferred future for you.

It is the difference between whether you will live a life of mere head belief in God or a transformed life of radically obedient heart behavior for God.

Fear is the enemy that stands in the way of our faith. In order to grow in faith we have to push through our fears.

FACED WITH A CHOICE

So God placed his people in a no way out, anxiety raising, fear producing situation. You heard it right. *God* placed them there.

> *When Pharaoh let the people go, God did not lead them on the road through the Philistine country, though that was shorter. For God said, "If they face war, they might change their minds and return to Egypt." So God led the people around by the desert road toward the Red Sea. The Israelites went up out of Egypt armed for battle. (Exodus 13:17-18)*

Question: What kind of a God would lead his people into a trap with no apparent way out? What kind of a God would send a bass boat up against a battleship? A kid on a tricycle up against a tank?

Answer: A God who wants to transform his people into warriors. Oh, they come out "armed for battle" all right. They are marching in army divisions. They think they can take on anyone in war. But God leads them away from physical battle until they have time to deal with the enemies of the heart.

Their minds had to be changed. They thought like slaves. In a moment's notice they were ready to bow down and cower to forces they knew well. They had to change their thinking and become warriors.

Their wills had to be changed. They had weak wills. At the first sign of trouble they would be ready to drop God's will for them and adopt the culture's will around them if it meant an easier path.

Their hearts had to be changed. They had fickle hearts. They had no real faith in God. As long as the exodus experiment was going smoothly, they were happy campers. But they were journeying with a faith that was hollow.

They were armed for battle, but becoming a warrior involves more than carrying a sword. So God leads them into a situation they cannot get out of without a total transformation.

It's the kind of transformation Alejandro needed in the movie *The Mask of Zorro*. The evil Don Rafael Montero ruled the land. The good Don Diego deLavega was defeated by him early in life. Montero even took DeLavega's young daughter and raised her as his own.

When DeLavega meets Alejandro, Alejandro is a young wild man. DeLavega invites him to train with him to be the next Zorro. Alejandro also nurses a grudge against Montero and pledges to kill him because one of Montero's soldiers had killed his brother.

In one scene don Diego is watching Alejandro as he trains. He is swinging his sword around wildly. He is ranting about how he will kill Montero. Zorro points to the sword in Alejandro's hand and says, "Do you know how to use that?" Alejandro confidently responds, "Yes." He raises the sword into the air and says, "The pointy end goes into the other man, no?"

Later, don Diego whips out his sword and spanks the sword out of Alejandro's untrained hand. He says, "This is going to take some work. You will fight bravely...and die." These are not the words Alejandro wants to hear. To his credit he chooses to submit to the training with Zorro and becomes gifted at the sword. Alejandro becomes the new Zorro.

The Israelites were armed but not trained to fight. They had to deal first with the enemies of the heart. God knew that if they faced the fierce Philistines at that time their minds would change, their wills would wilt, and their hearts would long for Egypt. Instead of taking them on the two and a half second journey from here to there, he takes them to the Red Sea. He leads them on the longer journey of transformation.

You may be familiar with that journey yourself. You wanted the shortest, most comfortable, most direct route. But what you couldn't see were the enemies ahead waiting to ambush your untrained soul. So God led you to other battles first.

Fear of a bad grade puts you in a position to cheat on a test. Will fear guide you, or will faith that God's path of honesty is the way out?

Fear of what people might think of you puts you in a position to rationalize and deny. Will fear guide you, or will faith that God's path of confession is the way out?

Fear of rejection pushes you to follow the crowd. Will fear guide you, or will faith that God's path of holiness is the way out?

Fear can drive you back into your old slaveries. Fear began to steer the Israelites back to theirs.

> *As Pharaoh approached, the Israelites looked up, and there were the Egyptians, marching after them. They were terrified and cried out to the* Lord. *They said to Moses, "Was it because there were no graves in Egypt that you brought us to the desert to die? What have you done to us by bringing us out of Egypt? Didn't we say to you in Egypt, 'Leave us alone; let us serve the Egyptians'? It would have been better for us to serve the Egyptians than to die in the desert!"* (Exodus 14:10-12)

Fear can scare the faith out of us. It did the Israelites. Sea on one side. Six elite armies on the other. They were scared...faithless. Instead of faith in God they begin to react out of their fear-induced anxiety.

"You haven't taken care of us. You never meant anything but harm for us."

"You don't know what's best for us."

"Slavery was better than this. My sin was better than this. My addiction was better than this."

Ever said similar snippets to God? It's at that moment you have to push through your fear to find faith. Fear is all about *you*. Faith is all about *God*. And the transformation God was looking for was faith. At times we need a Red Sea experience where we can see no way out so that we will look for God. At the Red Sea there was no way out unless God provided one.

STILL SEEING

So Moses told the people: "Do not be afraid. Stand firm and you will see the deliverance the LORD will bring you today. The Egyptians you see today you will never see again. The LORD will fight for you; you need only to be still" (Exodus 14:13-14).

The people stood still. And when they did, they saw.

They saw the angel of God move between the Israelites and the Egyptians.

They saw Moses raise his staff.

They saw God send a strong east wind that turned the water into dry land.

They saw a way opened up by God for them.

Which is exactly what he has promised to do for you. The apostle Paul writes in 1 Corinthians 10:13: "No temptation has seized you except what is common to man. And God is faithful; he will not let you be tempted beyond what you can bear. But when you are tempted, he will also provide a way out so that you can stand up under it."

Can you immediately see the way out? Many times not. The Israelites didn't. Notice the wind was an "east wind" (Exodus 14:21). All night long the wind blew from the east to the west. From the far side of the Red Sea to the Israelite side. All night long it was parting the waters until finally, in an instant, the last section of water parted and the way through was seen in its entirety.

God promises to do the same for you. But you have a choice. You can let your fear cause you to move around in a frenzied motion, doing things your way instead of God's. Or you can stand still in faith and look for his way out.

You won't have to look far. You have only to look as far as Jesus to find it. A statue of him gave Felix a place to stand and jump in faith. You can stand on the reality of him as your way out. In Luke 9 Jesus takes Peter, James and John up on a mountain with him to pray. Then..."Two men, Moses and Elijah, appeared in glorious splendor, talking with Jesus. They spoke about his departure...." (Luke 9:30-31).

His *departure* had to do with his exit from this life. His *departure* had to do with his death in Jerusalem. But it was a death followed by a resurrection to life. The Greek word for *departure* is translated as *exodus*. Jesus' exodus is ours. We follow him into:

A departure from old ways of thinking to God's way.

A departure from following our will to following God's.

A departure from acting out of fear to acting out of faith.

But we have to choose faith over fear. Those who do become warriors, defined by their trust in a God who shows them the way and stands between them and the enemy.

That's where the Israelites came out. They wanted to get from here to there and they did.

"Here" they entered the seabed as slaves. "There" they came out as believers.

"Here" they were unsure of God's ability to protect. "There" they were in awe of God's power to open up the sea.

"Here" they were frozen in fear because of the oncoming enemy. "There" they were founded in faith because God had dramatically come to protect them.

And as the last Egyptian was swallowed up in the sea, they began to see. And when they saw they sang.

> *I will sing to the LORD,*
> *for he is highly exalted.*
> *The horse and rider*
> *He has hurled into the sea.*
> *The LORD is my strength and my song;*
> *he has become my salvation.*
> *He is my God, and I will praise him,*
> *My father's God, and I will exalt him.*
> *The LORD is a warrior. (Exodus 15:1-3)*

Seasoned veterans of war will tell you that until you are more scared of your drill sergeant than the enemy, you aren't ready for combat. The people of Israel were no longer terrified of the Egyptians. They feared the LORD.

The Israelites fought the enemies of their heart and found victory. But it didn't come from their power. It was all about God. And, for a few moments at least, their witness became all about God.

Yours will too. Fight the enemies of your heart. Stand still on his mighty right hand. When he opens the way, jump. Your battle cry will be "the LORD is a warrior" all the way to the escape he has waiting for you below.

But it's either fear or faith. You choose.

The Israelites said to them, "If only we had died by the LORD's hand in Egypt! There we sat around pots of meat and ate all the food we wanted, but you have brought us out into this desert to starve this entire assembly to death."

EXODUS 16:3

Then the LORD said to Moses, "I will rain down bread from heaven for you."

EXODUS 16:4

The LORD said to Moses, "I have heard the grumbling of the Israelites. Tell them, 'At twilight you will eat meat, and in the morning you will be filled with bread. Then you will know that I am the Lord your God.'"

EXODUS 16:11-12

FILE 8

EXPECTING RAIN

EXODUS 16:2-15

You didn't notice it at first. At first it was just one day. But then one turned into two. Two turned into three. Three turned into four. You get the picture. Before long you are counting weeks, not days. Months, not weeks.

Reminders are everywhere. The grass crunches when you step on it. The sun burns you when you walk under it. The forecast disheartens you when you hear it. *No relief in sight.* The rain that you once took for granted now dominates your thoughts. You would give anything for a downpour to cool the air and water the crops.

We didn't grow up during the Dust Bowl era. But West Texas is familiar territory. We can remember times when rain was as sparse as the hair on a man with a shaved head. Lake levels were dangerously low. Water coming out of the faucet was brown. We were less concerned about watering our yards than we were about having water to drink.

The lack of moisture in the air left plenty of room for anxiety. People were tense. People began to grumble. They kept expecting rain. They kept getting drought. And when we get something different than what we expect it is human nature to grumble.

A beautiful young woman looks into the eyes of her handsome prince and says, "I do." They have made promises to each other for a lifetime of love. But, a few years down the road she finds herself on the verge of divorce. She did not get what she expected.

A man in his late thirties takes a job in another city. The pay is the same as his previous job, but the living expenses in the new location are higher. He and his wife have prayed and believed that it is God's will for them to make the move. His employer has even told him there would be a raise in a few months if he would come. The "few months" come and the raise doesn't. The man finds himself with a loss of trust in his employer and a tightening of the budget belt at home. He did not get what he expected.

A couple prays for the gift of a child. They patiently wait for the day that God will give them the news they so hopefully want to hear. Finally, that day arrives and plans and preparations for this child's arrival are begun. Anticipations climb higher and higher, only to be dashed against the sharp crags below as they find that their child will not be born healthy. They definitely did not get what they expected.

A single person with a good salary and good looks continues to return home every evening by herself. She lives a highly productive life. She has most anything a woman her age could want, except a husband. She brings her prayers to God night after night, only to awaken each morning to the reality that she is still single. She believes God answers prayers, but her prayers begin to pale as she pushes her mid-thirties. She has not received what she expected.

What we often get is not what we expected. When we want rain and get drought we find ourselves in a desert.

HUNGRY FOR GOD

That's where the Israelites were: in the desert. Metaphorically, they needed rain. Literally, they needed food. They had just survived a water crisis. After three days of wilderness wandering they found water at Marah (Exodus 15:22-27). They expected a cool, refreshing drink. What they got was a bitter taste in their mouth. Next thing you know they were grumbling. "What are we to drink?" they ask. Only a short time has passed since they walked on dry land with a wall of water on each side, yet they grumble against Moses.

Being the leader that he was, Moses has no one to cry out to but God. God directs him to throw a piece of wood in the water. Strange thing to do. But his obedience opened the way for the water to be made sweet. Seven miles down the road they discover where God was leading them all along. *Elim*. The tourist billboard read: "Home of twelve springs and seventy palm trees".

From there they set out to another desert—the Desert of Sin. They had just been camping out by water Ozarka would have bottled. Their expectations were high. "This is what life following God will be like!" Now all they could see was desert. And—you guessed it—they grumbled.

This time it was because of food. Their stomachs rumble and they begin to grumble. They think they are starving to death. "If only we had died by the Lord's hand in Egypt! There we sat around pots of meat and ate all the food we wanted, but you have brought us out into this desert to starve this entire assembly to death" (Exodus 16:3). They expected food. They wanted dessert but all they got was desert. What they think they have is famine. Egypt was behind them. The Promised Land somewhere in front of them.

Kids are prone to grumbling. One wants the computer but the other one is already on it. One wants to watch one show but the other already is watching another. One wants to mow the lawn for his Dad but the other has beaten him to it. (We can dream a little, can't we?)

Their grumbling does not bring out the best in us. We fathers ask questions like:

"Do you like your room? Good! That's all you're going to see for about a week!"

"How old are you? 13? Wonderful! Do you want to see 14?"

"Why do you favor your mother so much?"

When kids grumble we tend to want to respond in like manner. That's what happens when people grumble. Like thunder rumbling through the clouds, a rumble spreads from one person to the next. Teeth are clenched and a low *grrrr* is let out. The effect is contagious as it spreads through the camp. *Grrrummbblle*.

You'd expect God to react in a similar manner. You'd expect him to send the Israelites right back to Egypt. They deserved the kind of reception they would get from Pharaoh. God has been good to them. He's delivered them. Shown them incredible power. He's lived up to every promise he's made them so far. And now they grumble. They expected one thing and think they've got another.

The lesson of the Wilderness is that you don't always get what you expect. That can be devastating news if you are traveling the Wilderness alone. But if you are following God it can be life-altering news. You'd expect him to give these ungracious grumblers just what they deserve. Match their ungraciousness with ungraciousness. Instead, he matches their ungraciousness with his grace.

As he's done all through Exodus, he hears their grumbling (16:7). The grumbling isn't just against Moses and Aaron. It's against God. (We might do well to note that God takes grumbling against his leaders personally.) And so we might expect his reaction to be harsh.

But God's purpose for leading this group into the Wilderness is not to beat them up for their mistakes. His purpose is found in Exodus 16:11: "I have heard the grumbling of the Israelites. Tell them, 'At twilight you will eat meat, and in the morning you will be filled with bread. Then you will know that I am the Lord your God.'"

God takes his children—grumbling and all—and shapes them into his people. He hears their dry cries of disillusionment, their thirsty cries of fear, their hungry cries of disbelief. And he answers. He answers by sending rain to their parched and barren souls.

HEAVENLY RAIN

"I will rain down bread from heaven for you" (Exodus 16:4). In the middle of their Wilderness, God sends rain.

The first time God sent rain is found in Genesis 7. The people didn't know what was happening. Imagine Noah telling the people—who had never seen rain before—that it was going to rain. "Rain? What's that?" they asked. Until the rain, the land had only been watered by a mist that came up from the ground. Noah hammered and they harassed. Noah nailed and they needled. Then one day the skies opened up. It rained. And the people didn't know what hit them. It was something new. Something they hadn't expected.

Something new happened here too. God sent food in the evening and in the morning (Exodus 16:6-7). The order is important. The order recalls creation language (see Genesis 1:5 ff.). God is creating something new. In the Wilderness, when it looks as if there is no way out, when we don't get what we expect, faith says that God will create something new.

For the Israelites, he created manna. It looked like frosted flakes (16:14). The people don't know what it is, so they call it *manna*. It is the same expression you've used when you arrive home to find that your husband has been experimenting in the kitchen again. The table is spread and the main dish is uncovered. You take a bite. Your husband looks at you expectantly and asks, "What do you think?" You feel a bit risky. You put your life on the line by asking back, "What is it?" You have just identified your meal as manna, or, "what is it?"

For you and me, we might ask the same: "*What is it? What is it* that God is going to do? *What is it* that he will do when we don't get what we expected in life? *What is it* God will do when we find ourselves in the Wilderness?"

If you are following God you will have Wilderness experiences. *You have wilderness experiences because you have faith.* You probably expected us to say you have wilderness experiences because of a *lack* of faith. But the only reason the Israelites found themselves in the Wilderness is that they followed God by faith. Their problem and ours is that we don't often get what we expect.

Too many televangelists have taught the Christian world to believe that God is found mainly in the extraordinary experiences. And so that is what we expect. The Israelites had seen the power in the plagues, the water of walls as they passed through the Red Sea, and the bitter water turned to sweet. They were beginning to look for God only in their great expectations.

So God sends rain. Not merely a drop or a sprinkle. He sends a full-blown gully washer of *bread from heaven*. Quail in the evening. Manna in the morning.

> Quail flying in from Africa or blown in from the Mediterranean are often exhausted enough to be flying low and can be caught by hand. The manna could have been a natural phenomenon in the Sinai Peninsula. A type of plant lice punctures the fruit of the tamarisk tree and excretes a substance from this juice, a yellowish-white flake or ball. During the warmth of the day it disintegrates, but it congeals when it is cold. It has a sweet taste. Rich in carbohydrates and sugar, it is still gathered by natives, who bake it into a kind of bread (and call it manna). The food decays quickly and attracts ants.[1]

Some contend that God was taking ordinary occurrences and blessing his people with them. If this is how God chose to send rain to his people, he still caused it to happen. And if so, there may have been a greater miracle: the miracle to help us see that God is with us in the ordinary and everyday.

A good night's sleep.

A healthy diet.

Honest work.

Relaxing play on the Sabbath.

If we fail to see God in the ordinary, we might miss him altogether. Many have.

Another time he "rained down bread from heaven" was in the form of his Son Jesus. The people were grumbling then too (John 6:41, 43). "I am the bread of life," he said (John 6:48). And many missed it.

They missed it because they expected a sign but got the Son. "What miraculous sign then will you give that we may see it and believe you?" (John 6:30).

They missed it because they expected the unusual but got the familiar. “Is this not Jesus, the son of Joseph, whose father and mother we know?” (John 6:42).

They missed it because they expected the material but got the Messiah. “How can this man give us his flesh to eat?” (John 6:52).

God has rained down bread from heaven for us. When we see him we may have the same reaction. *What is it?* So new. So ordinary. But when we get up each day and believe in him, we will have all we need for that day.

We may just find more than we expected.

Is the Lord among us or not?

EXODUS 17:7

FILE 9

QUESTIONS FROM THE BACKSEAT

EXODUS 17:1-7

Every parent has been there.

The trip ahead is long. The travel schedule is tight. You hit the road with a full tank and swelled head that the plan you have produced beats anything AAA could muster.

But twenty minutes down the highway you hear a small, squeaky voice from the backseat. "Can we stop? I have to go to the bathroom." Inside you go ballistic. "Didn't she take care of that before we left?" Outside you calmly respond to your wife, "I'll see what I can find, honey."

Your keen eye finds a Stop-N-Go in record time. (At least the name fits your plans.) As your family takes care of business you visit with the owner. "We only need the bathroom. Just left home a half hour ago. We've got ten hours of traveling today." The owner just smiles as he peers over your shoulder and sees the rest of your family stocking up on snacks and 16 oz. Big Gulps.

Back in your vehicle you and your spouse assume your stations at command central—the front seat. It's a battle you are determined to win: get to your destination by dusk. But before you make it past the next outpost you are bombarded with incoming artillery. It's what you feared most and prepared least for. The questions.

Some you expected.

"Are we there yet?"

"How much longer?"

"Can we get something to eat?"

Others blindside you.

"Why is there a light in the 'frigerator and not in the freezer?"

"How come Goofy stands while Pluto stays on all fours?"

"Did you know the Alphabet song and "Twinkle, Twinkle Little Star" have the same tune?"

You stop singing in your head just in time to take shrapnel from the next volley.

"Who was the first person to decide to squeeze those things on a cow and drink whatever came out?"

"Why does our dog get mad at us when we blow in his face but when we take him on a car ride he sticks his head out the window?"

Every parent has been there. Questions from the backseat. You come to expect them. Every journey includes them. The same is true for the journey of faith.

SETTING OUT

In Exodus 17:1 the whole Israelite community "set out." It's a theme of their journey (see Exodus 16:1 and 19:2). God's people are a people on the way, setting out from one place to the next as the LORD commands.

"Where" his people are going is not the main question. "Who" they are going with is. There is no "instant faith" packed for this trip. Faith is something that is picked up along the way. It is built in the journey. It grows as you travel down the road. It matures along the way. And you won't find it unless you "set out."

God takes his place in the front seat and lets the questions begin. The Israelites camp at one place for awhile. About the time they get comfortable, he says, "Load 'em up. It's time to move on."

Each time God moves in the pillar of fire or the column of cloud they have a choice. Will they load up and follow or will they stay put? Faith brought them this far. Will it be enough to force them to move on? Or will they get complacent and decide that where they are is good enough?

Hard to imagine anyone deciding to stay when God moves isn't it? Maybe not. We do the same. Just like kids on a trip we get tired of the journey. We want to know when we can stop.

We get tired of serving.

We get tired of waiting.

We get tired of the people we're traveling with.

But until we get to the destination we have to keep going. We may stop for a short rest or time to stretch the legs. But at some point the driver will say, "Let's go." And so we set out.

The faith journey is just that. *A journey. Movement.* It is a series of setting out moments. For the Israelites it meant literally moving from one geographic scenic spot to the next on their way to the land of promise. For us it means a spiritual journey that takes us from one level of faith to the next.

But you have to keep moving. And faith is the fuel that takes us from one stop on the journey to the next. Your faith will only be refueled if you choose to go.

ROADBLOCKS

Roadblocks may appear on the journey in the form of questions. Questions surface because we would rather travel by sight instead of faith. Consider the newly married couple. The husband is the careful one. Before a trip he takes out the map, plots the stopping points, procures the money, and packs the clothes.

The wife, on the other hand, is the carefree one. She loves the adventure of traveling. "Let's just go! We'll figure it out on the way" is more her style. "We'll get money on the way. Don't worry about packing many clothes. We can always buy some new ones on the trip." (About three years into the marriage he catches on.)

Years later their ways of traveling merge into one. They pack lighter. They trust they will find what they need. He even learns to go to Wal-Mart without first checking the city map.

The questions can stop you before you ever set out. At times they almost halted the Israelites. They faced faith roadblocks on their journey because they wanted sight. They wanted to know what was out there first. They got hit with a bad case of the "whaddifs?" and "wonderifs?"

"Whaddif we made a mistake coming out here?"

"Whaddif Moses doesn't know what he's doing?"

"Wonderif we should just go back?"

Backseat questions that sound familiar? God calls us through his leaders today and we launch a volley of "whaddifs?" and "wonderifs?" ourselves.

"Whaddif we make a mistake?"

"Wonderif we should just keep walking the same way we used to?"

"Whaddif the leaders don't know what they're doing?"

Questions. All based in fear, not faith. Paved in a desire for sight, not trust. But these are only off ramps from the real question of the journey. We find it in Exodus 17:7.

"Is the Lord among us or not?"

That's the real roadblock the Israelites face. They find themselves in the middle of the wilderness and they want to know if God is with them or not. Don't be too quick to judge them. Why shouldn't they ask the question? The wilderness looks like a godforsaken place, doesn't it?

But it isn't. God is leading them. But he leads them to some places we would not choose. He takes them to a place in the wilderness where there is no water. No Stop-N-Go. You'd think he would lead them to an oasis. Instead he pulls over at a waterless place.

God is in the driver's seat. We are in the backseat. And we have to admit that some of his stops can make us question. We can question whether or not God is really among us.

When people disappoint us, we question.

When we think we're doing what God wants but have difficulty seeing results, we question.

When other churches are growing but ours isn't, we question.

When people we pray for don't get better, we question.

When hearts don't soften to God's loving-kindness, we question.

When homes don't heal, we question.

When people continue to struggle with obedience, we question.

Haven't you questioned whether God is really among us or not? You wonder why you feel so bad when God is so good. You wonder why some seem to understand the message so easily when you only get confused.

Maybe your questions have left you feeling guilty. And if you think God is upset with you because you question, you didn't learn that from this text. Notice what happens. The people are questioning whether God is among them or not. They demand an answer. They want sight.

THE DRINK STOP

"Give us water to drink" (Exodus 17:2).

If you return to their first water crisis they politely asked, "What are we to drink?" (Exodus 15:24). Now they demand. And deep below the surface of the demand is the question: "Is the Lord among us or not?"

They're getting a little testy, so they test God. They "put him to the proof." That is why this place comes to be called *Massah* (Exodus 17:7). It's a place of testing. They were saying they would not believe God unless he showed himself to them in some concrete way. And they name the way. "Make water materialize."

We get a little testy too on the journey and test God ourselves.

We throw caution to the wind and expect God to protect us.

We spend more than we bring in and expect God to rescue us.

We ignore relationship rules God has given us and expect our marriages and friendships to thrive anyway.

We plan first and pray that God will bless our plan later instead of praying first and planning after God speaks.

We put God to the test. We want to exchange the backseat for the front. And that makes for a long journey. God can handle our doubts. He can handle our questions. We suspect he expects them.

But when we put ourselves in the driver's seat God has to correct us. It happened here in the wilderness. It happened in Jesus' ministry.

Jesus was explaining to his disciples how he would go to Jerusalem and be killed on the cross. Peter was tired of sitting in the backseat so he took Jesus aside and rebuked him. It's a wonder Jesus didn't turn him into ashes right there. But he didn't. What he did do is tell him to get back where he was supposed to be. Behind him (Mark 8:32-33).

And it's a wonder God didn't leave the Israelites right there. But he didn't. Instead he gave Moses some instructions. "Walk on ahead of the people," he tells Moses. Then he adds, "I will stand there *before* you."

God puts everyone back where they need to be. It is the proper approach to the journey. God leads his leaders who in turn lead his people.

And he does much more. He gives them grace. It's not what they deserved, but it's what they got. He didn't respond to them because they put him to the test. He had nothing to prove. He had proven himself over and over again already on this journey of faith.

He responded because of love. He gave them water.

He'll give you water too, even when you don't deserve it. He can handle the questions you have on the journey. He can put up with the grumbling.

As long as we keep walking. Pick up your questions and follow. Each step of the way. Until you look up and see him *before* you.

That's when you will know you have arrived.

In the third month after the Israelites left Egypt—on the very day—they came to the Desert of Sinai. After they set out...they entered the Desert of Sinai, and Israel camped there in the desert in front of the mountain.

Then Moses went up to God, and the LORD *called to him from the mountain and said, "This is what you are to say to the house of Jacob and what you are to tell the people of Israel: 'You yourselves have seen what I did to Egypt, and how I carried you on eagles' wings and brought you to myself. Now if you obey me fully and keep my covenant, then out of all nations you will be my treasured possession. Although the whole earth is mine, you will be for me a kingdom of priests and a holy nation.' These are the words you are to speak to the Israelites."*

EXODUS 19:1-6

FILE 10

MEETING GOD ON THE MOUNTAIN

EXODUS 19:1-24:11

In 1988 I (Reg) spent fifteen days in the Holy Land, the land of promise God's people in Exodus are journeying towards.

Moving from Israel to Egypt is an experience in extremes. One night we were staying in the Camp David Hotel in Tel Aviv on the shores of the Mediterranean. The Camp David Hotel is a five-story, luxury hotel. The workers at the hotel come to your room at night while you're out at dinner or sightseeing and carefully lay out your sleeping clothes from your suitcase.

My set up must have been a shock. All I had taken for luggage was a backpack and all I slept in was a T-shirt and shorts. I can just imagine the guy who got sent to my room looking for sleeping clothes. "Where's his pajamas?!" For the whole trip I had taken only two T-shirts. A blue one and a red one. I washed them with backpacking soap at night in the hotel bathrooms, dried them on a towel, and hung them to dry. So you can imagine how uncomfortable I was with all of that first-class treatment at this posh hotel.

The transition into the wilderness is a bit shocking. The next morning they loaded us on a bus and we headed south towards Egypt. We traveled through the Negev desert where the exodus took place. We got out at a gas station halfway through the long day's drive and were greeted by 127 degrees of "knock you down" hot.

That evening we pulled up to St. Catherine's monastery. This monastery was built in 565 AD, sits at the foot of Mt. Sinai, and is virtually untouched.

That night we sat on the floor to eat in a room where camels were tied up outside. Bare bulbs were screwed into the wall. The difference in lodging accommodations couldn't have been more extreme.

We arose at 2:00 AM to climb the mountain of God. Our non-English speaking guide led us sans flashlight through the rocky terrain under the faint glow of star light. It's a 5,000 foot vertical climb to the top of the 7,482 foot mountain, and each step was felt more than visualized.

We summitted the peak at the first hint of dawn and were immediately greeted by an uninhibited view of hundreds of miles of granite-peaked wilderness which showed not one sign of human occupation. Little would appear different to our eyes than it had appeared to Moses' eyes thousands of years ago. I stood there bewildered and tried for the life of me to eternally etch the memory of what I was seeing into my soul. I'll never be the same. What an introduction to the mountain of God!

SUMMIT DESTINATIONS

When the Israelites left Egypt, they had one destination in mind. The Promised Land.

When the Israelites left Egypt, God had one destination in mind. Mt. Sinai.

> *In the third month after the Israelites left Egypt—on the very day—they came to the Desert of Sinai. After they set out...they entered the Desert of Sinai, and Israel camped there in the desert in front of the mountain. (Exodus 19:1-2)*

To some, Mt. Sinai may look like nothing more than a mere pile of rocks. But to the people of God, it is a spiritual location. It is a weather-beaten precipice with faith altering power. It is a holy spire which sits on holy ground. It is designed by God with one thing in mind.

Revelation.

Mt. Sinai was configured by God so he could communicate to and touch the hearts of his people. That has always been God's goal. Human hearts. He will craft a mountain, shape a seashore, or erect a cross if that's what it takes to get our attention and alter our eternity. And he hasn't changed. His desire to touch the hearts of his people is still his burning desire today.

The rescue and release of the people from Egypt was just a prelude to the true plans of God. God has something wonderful designed for the hearts of his people. He did then and he does now.

If you believe that, then don't let the long trek in the wilderness distract you from God's ultimate destination for your life. Don't doubt the love of Jesus when answers or changes don't come quick and easy.

Remember that God did not break you out of your Egypt so that you could find a comfortable corner of the church to sit back in. God is equipping you to become a warrior. And the equipment you need is found on the mountain of God. In Exodus 19 we hear straight from God why he took his people to Sinai:

> *Then Moses went up to God, and the* LORD *called to him from the mountain and said, "This is what you are to say to the house of Jacob and what you are to tell the people of Israel: 'You yourselves have seen what I did to Egypt, and how I carried you on eagles' wings and brought you to myself. Now if you obey me fully and keep my covenant, then out of all nations you will be my treasured possession. Although the whole earth is mine, you will be for me a kingdom of priests and a holy nation.' These are the words you are to speak to the Israelites." (Exodus 19:3-6)*

MOUNTAINTOP ENCOUNTERS

Mountaintop encounters with God will always reveal two things. First, they reveal something about God. Second, they reveal something about you.

Mt. Sinai was no exception. Camped out in the desert of Sinai on a stretch of land two miles long and a half mile wide, looking up at the summit towering 5,000 feet above their heads, the people's perspective of God would rise as high as the peaks before them while their view of themselves would be stretched as far as the land around them.

On the mountain God reveals something about himself. He has a passionate, pursuing, possessive love for his people.

His *passionate* love is apparent. He heard his people's cries. He saw their trouble. He could have responded like the Deists' God. He could have stayed at a distance and let things work out for themselves. But he didn't. Passion would not allow him to. And so he entered their bondage and his people exited Egypt.

His *pursuing* love is persistent. Notice the imagery. "I carried you on eagles' wings and brought you to myself" (Exodus 19:4). An eagle soars high above the earth, eyes keenly trained on the terrain below. Searching and scouring the scenery until it selects specifically what it desires. Then suddenly it swoops down and scoops up the prize for itself. God saw, searched, and snatched the Hebrew people out of Egypt for himself.

God's *possessive* love is plain.

- "brought you to *myself*"
- "*my* treasured possession"
- "you will be *for me*"

What kind of love would go to such lengths? A *transforming* love. The God encountered on mountaintops is a God who takes slaves and gives them freedom. He is a God who takes orphans and gives them homes. He is a God who finds those who don't belong and brings them to himself as his belongings.

His people longed for a homeland. God longed to bring the people to the heartland of his love. The LORD who rescued them, the God who acted mightily for them, the Creator who drew them out of a life of slavery is the same one who loved them perfectly. His transformation of their character could never be accomplished outside of this intimate, loving relationship.

THE BLESSING OF GOD

Any loving relationship has the power to free those in the relationship for true love. A relationship with God is no different. So he speaks Ten Words at the summit that have forever defined God's people. The first four defined their relationship with him.

God declares his name and deeds, and demands exclusive rights to their hearts. "No other gods" (Exodus 20:3).

He demands that no earthly image be made to depict his presence. Any attempt would be degrading. No other "god" ever demanded this. "No images" (Exodus 20:4).

His name is so sacred and holy it is only to be used seriously. To bring his name into any situation is to render that situation HOLY! "No misuse of his name" (Exodus 20:7).

The relationship is so crucial it reserves a day a week where one stops from mindless activity and becomes mindful of God. "Remember the Sabbath and keep it holy" (Exodus 20:8).

God gives his people the building blocks to become the great nation he promised. *His* great nation. Take a look at what would happen if the people seriously invested in the relationship.

> *If you listen carefully...and do all that I say, I will be an enemy to your enemies and will oppose those who oppose you. My angel will go ahead of you and bring you into the land of the Amorites, Hittites, Perizzites, Canaanites, Hivites and Jebusites, and I will wipe them out. Do not bow down before their gods or worship them or follow their practices. You must demolish them and break their sacred stones to pieces. Worship the LORD your God, and his*

> *blessing will be on your food and water. I will take away sickness from among you, and none will miscarry or be barren in your land. I will give you a full life span. I will send my terror ahead of you and throw into confusion every nation you encounter. I will make all your enemies turn their backs and run.* (Exodus 23:22-27)

These rules did not separate God from his people.

These rules removed barriers to relationship so that God could offer a relationship that leads to uninhibited intimacy.

These rules offered God's people a relationship that leads to unparalleled blessings. "I will make you into a great nation and I will bless you."

When you meet God on the mountain he reveals that he is a God who is in passionate pursuit of you to possess you so that you may possess his blessings.

And we like blessings, don't we? We want to be blessed. And God wants to bless us. But he wants to bless us for a purpose. When we look for the blessing and stop the process when we receive it, God's purpose for us and his world have not been fulfilled.

Read carefully the following words from Brian McLaren. He divides the Abrahamic call (Genesis 12:2) into two clauses: "Clause A"—"I will make your name great, and you will be a blessing;" and "Clause B"—"all peoples on earth will be blessed through you."

> Lesslie Newbigin often spoke of the greatest heresy of monotheism (in its Jewish, Christian, and Islamic forms): cherishing Clause A of the Abrahamic call while conveniently suppressing, forgetting, or ignoring Clause B. So, we want to be blessed (big, exciting, vibrant, wealthy, healthy, wise). We want to be great (a great nation, a great denomination, a great congregation). To this end we pray and pay and read and plead and strive and strain and yearn and learn and groan and labor. And we give birth to wind.[1]

But God doesn't. He gives birth to nations. His destination is Sinai, a mountaintop meeting where he reveals to his people a new view of who he is.

THE BLESSING OF OTHERS

On the mountain he also reveals a new view of you. That revelation is found in the second set of words he speaks at the mountain.

"Honor your father and mother" (Exodus 20:12).

"You shall not murder" (Exodus 20:13).

"You shall not commit adultery" (Exodus 20:14).

"You shall not steal" (Exodus 20:15).

"You shall not give false testimony against your neighbor" (Exodus 20:16).

"You shall not covet...anything that belongs to your neighbor" (Exodus 20:17).

The very survival of society rests on the fact that family, all human life, marriage, property and justice is sacred. And it all stems from a sacred inner attitude that belongs to God. Because we have intimacy with God we have a new impetus, goal, and guide for relationships with one another.

We want the blessings. So why not *just* the blessings? Why does God have to direct his laws from loving him to loving those we encounter everyday? Because he is a God who does not stop at the first clause. He moved quickly into the second: "I will make your name great, and you will be a blessing....and all peoples on earth will be blessed through you."

God had said it even before he spoke the Ten Words. "You will be for me a kingdom of priests and a holy nation" (Exodus 19:6). They are no longer to be wanderers. They are no longer to be slaves. They are no longer to live for themselves. They are to be priests. They are to be blessed to be a blessing.

And so are we. We are to be priests who bless others. A true mountaintop experience with God is holy and will reveal to you something about yourself: there is a holy purpose to your life. You are to be a priest. Now before you collapse or put on a collar, pay attention to four things ancient priests in Israel did.

They made sacrifices prescribed by the law. The sacrifices provided a way for sinful people to come into communion with a holy God. Without the sacrifices no relationship could occur. Priests provide passageways for others into intimacy with God.

They communicated God's law to the people. God's law offered direction for daily decisions. This law from the Creator would keep the created from becoming entrapped in sin and from losing connection with each other and God. Priests kept the passageway open through diligent communication offering direction to directionless people.

They served as judges to solve difficult disputes. All humans experience conflict. Priests brought God's wisdom into all areas of social contact with the impact of freeing people from bitterness and directing them towards joy and peace.

And finally, *they enhanced the spiritual health of the nation.* The priest actually held the nation together. In fact, if the nation sinned, part of the blame is laid on its spiritual leadership. Without powerful spiritual leadership the nation was doomed!

"What?! Are you implying that if there are problems in our nation the solution may start with the people of God?" You got that exactly right! It starts with his priests. In 2 Chronicles 7:14, the LORD tells Solomon there will be a time when the condition of the land will take a turn south. He then tells the king what can be done to set in motion the healing of the land.

> *If my people, who are called by my name, will humble themselves and pray and seek my face and turn from their wicked ways, then will I hear from heaven and will forgive their sin and will heal their land.*

God doesn't tell the government to get its legislation worked out. God doesn't tell the schools to get their curriculum straight. God doesn't tell

Hollywood to clean up their act. He tells his people to be the priests they were meant to be!

McLaren suggests that God is searching for people who have had a summit meeting with God and share his same desire to be a blessing.

> ...And we give birth to wind. Meanwhile, might God be otherwise occupied, scanning the earth for people who will also cherish Clause B: to be made into a great blessing, so that all people on earth can be blessed through us? Are we seeking blessing so as to be a blessing to the world God loves? Our persistent "bless-me" bug, like a nasty flu into which we keep relapsing, creates what some of my friends have called "the great commotion," a close approximation of the Great Commission, but a miss nonetheless. Seminar junkies accumulate plastic-covered notebooks that could fill an oil tanker. Authors like myself write books whose combined gross weight may exceed the weight of our congregations after a pot-luck dinner. But not much changes. Our efforts are all bent to renew or strengthen the current systems, which are perfectly designed (as Dallas Willard has said) to deliver the results we are now getting.
>
> So if we are a self-centered church in America, it is because our systems—including our theological systems—are perfectly designed to produce such a church. It has been said that the greatest obstacle to the coming of the kingdom of God is the church, preoccupied with her own existence. Could our preoccupation with making better churches rather than better blessing the world be the heart disease that plagues us? And could our Clause-A theological systems be the high-fat cause of that heart disease?[2]

MOUNTAINTOP MAKEOVERS

God's words are transforming words. And transformation is tough. Don't journey to the mountain lightly. It's a dangerous mountain with majestic power inhabiting its crags and crevices. Thunder. Lightning. Trumpets. Smoke. It's enough to make you shake in your boots in fear for your life.

And that's exactly what the Hebrews did.

> *When the people saw the thunder and lightning and heard the trumpet and saw the mountain in smoke, they trembled with fear. They stayed at a distance and said to Moses, "Speak to us yourself and we will listen. But do not have God speak to us or we will die." Moses said to the people, "Do not be afraid, God has come to test you, so that the fear of God will be with you to keep you from sinning." The people remained at a distance.... (Exodus 20:18-21)*

Can you believe that?! Immediately after God speaks his people ask that he not do it again! They want blessings, yes. But change? The words were too difficult to hear. So they "remained at a distance."

Men and women have remained at a distance from God ever since. Why is that? Good question. Here's an answer. Sinai is serious stuff. The mountain is transformational. Sinai is about coming face to face with who you are and who you were meant to be. And for most of us, there's a fairly large gap between the two.

But Sinai will not be ignored. God will get your attention. He will begin by reminding you of what kind of God you have. He is in passionate pursuit to possess you. He has heard your cries. The same God who carried the Israelites on eagle's wings has carried you.

And he has led you to another mountain. Mount Calvary. It is there he has defeated your enemies once again through the death of a firstborn son. This time his own.

He beckons you to feel the spikes piercing the flesh.

Hear his cries of agony.

Tremble in awe as this mountain also quakes.

Yes, tread up to the mountain and God will get your attention. Thunder. Lightning. Trumpets. Smoke. He will get your attention because he deserves your attention. Who other has done so much for you? What other "god" has rescued you? Who other loves you enough to reserve your heart only for himself?

None can stand in his presence for long without being transformed. His desire is to bless and he will have his way with you until you become a blessing for others. Priests. People who are preoccupied with bringing God's heart and healing to the land.

Your destination is not a land. It is not just to be blessed.

Your destination is the LORD. Rescued to become a rescuer. Healed to become a healer. It is to know the blessing of his presence in your life and in turn become a blessing to others.

Camp at the mountain and find yourself home where you were destined to be.

They came back to Moses and Aaron and the whole Israelite community at Kadesh in the Desert of Paran. There they reported to them and to the whole assembly and showed them the fruit of the land. They gave Moses this account: "We went into the land to which you sent us, and it does flow with milk and honey! Here is its fruit. But the people who live there are powerful, and the cities are fortified and very large. We even saw descendants of Anak there. The Amalekites live in the Negev; the Hittites, Jebusites and Amorites live in the hill country; and the Canaanites live near the sea and along the Jordan. Then Caleb silenced the people before Moses and said, "We should go up and take possession of the land, for we can certainly do it."

But the men who had gone up with him said, "We can't attack those people; they are stronger than we are." And they spread among the Israelites a bad report about the land they had explored.

NUMBERS 13:26-32

FILE 11

THE SPRING OF DECISION

EXODUS 15:22-17:16; NUMBERS 10, 13-15

Decision time.

You find it in the sports world. The shot clock shows five seconds. The score is tied. The lane is open. *It's decision time.*

You find it in the corporate world. Sales are slow. Profits are plummeting. Shareholders begin chanting for a change. *It's decision time.*

You find it in your world. Old habits hold you hostage. Deep change is knocking at your door. Fear can lock you inside or faith can open passageways to new life. It's decision time.

Decision time is the space between the time an opportunity surfaces and a direction is chosen. That space can be small—a matter of seconds. That space can be large—a matter of days or weeks or months. That time found in that space can be faced with fear or faith. But it must be faced. Hanging in the balance is often deep change or slow death.[1]

No way around it, the journey of life leads us repeatedly to decision time. The journey with God is no different.

DIRECTION DECISIONS

After Sinai the *habiru* found themselves in the wilderness. They knew who God was. He had revealed himself to them through Ten Words at the mountain. They also knew they had been called to be more than they had ever envisioned before.

They were faced with decision time. The question "Who are we?" is penetrating the deepest recesses of their being.

Egyptians or Israelites?

Slave or free?

Wanderers or warriors?

Fearful or faithful?

These followers of God are soul searching in the scorching desert of Sinai. An opportunity lies before them. It has been two years since they have left Egypt. From living with Pharaoh they have come to live with God. Every day the sight of the Tabernacle in the middle of their camp reminds them of this amazing revelation: *God lives with his people.*

They had left as slaves. They had left as broken people. And now they ponder the realization that the God who made short work of the "gods" of Egypt, the God who parted the Red Sea, the God who has performed mind-blowing miracles and demonstrated his passionate love for them is living in their midst. That knowledge and experience of his presence is transforming their identity.

But the real soul searching started with the calf.

While Moses was on the mountain the people made a decision. They wanted a god they could see. They melted down the gold and "out came a calf." Out came other nonsense as well. Revelry. Drunkenness. Even at Sinai sin surfaced.

Sin creates a meltdown in relationship. It becomes the master you obey instead of God. You begin to follow sin and step away from God. He doesn't step away from you. The result of your being ruled by slave thinking is separation from God.

Paul put it this way:

> *Don't you know that when you offer yourselves to someone to obey him as slaves, you are slaves to the one whom you obey—whether you are slaves to sin, which leads to death, or to obedience, which leads to righteousness? But thanks be to God that, though you used to be slaves to sin, you wholeheartedly obeyed the form of*

teaching to which you were entrusted. You've been set free from sin and have become slaves to righteousness. (Romans 6:16)

This hard-headed, obstinate group of followers had decided to be slaves to sin. They chose to go back to a slave mentality. Decision time sent them back to their old ways instead of forward to deep change. As Robert Quinn says,

> We do not tend to choose the healthy alternative. We actually seem to prefer slow death. Slow death is the devil we know, so we prefer it to the devil we do not know....Deep change requires discipline, courage, and motivation. We would rather experience the pain of slow death than the threat of changing ourself.[2]

The decision for slow death, to revert to the slave mentality, is costly. The Israelites spent eleven months at the foot of Mt. Sinai. Eight months of their stay came after receiving the law. Eight months during which every day they encountered reminders of the result of their decision.

The mountain reminded them of God's holiness.

Moses reminded them of God's steadfast word.

The tablets of stone reminded them of God's perfect law.

The tombs of friends and family destroyed by sin reminded them of the wage of sin.

The decision for slow death is costly.

Even still, God is in their midst. In his mercy he stays with these wanderers who are trying to answer the question, "Who are we?" Identity change takes time. Deep change always does. And so in this time of waiting God is preparing them and reorganizing them.

God shapes you in the wilderness of life like a blacksmith fashions his iron. He stretches your heart out across the anvil. He stokes the fires. He brings his hammer down. And the mettle of your life is forged by the loving hand of God. He is transforming you.

Pounding out the wanderer.

Shaping you into a warrior.

And leading you to decision time.

Mt. Sinai had served its purpose. Revelation. Now God had a new location in mind. Kadesh Barnea.

OASIS OF DECISIONS

> *On the twentieth day of the second month of the second year, the cloud lifted from above the tabernacle of the Testimony. Then the Israelites set out from the Desert of Sinai and traveled from place to place until the cloud came to rest in the Desert of Paran. They set out, this first time, at the Lord's command through Moses. The divisions of the camp of Judah went first, under their standard. (Numbers 10:11-14)*

When they left Egypt, this group of wanderers would have followed anyone to get away from the searing brick pits and the lash of the whip. They weren't following God as much as they were just getting out of Egypt.

Just like many of us. We read books or sit in churches not because we want to follow God. We just want to get away from sin punishment. We're much more interested in finding a way out of the mess we're in than we are in following anyone. We're not heading anywhere in particular...just leaving the ruin or boredom of the place we are now.

But God wants more for our lives than that. He wants our hearts. And he wanted theirs. So he let them spend months with nothing to focus on but desert, a mountain peak and his Words. The Ten Words that offered an invitation to relationship.

By the time they "set out" they must have thought, "This is it! To Canaan's land we're on our way." God thought differently. Instead of the place of promise he leads them to the place of decision. Kadesh Barnea.

Kadesh was first mentioned in Genesis 14. There it is known as *En Mishpat*. *En Mishpat* is an oasis in the desert. During the days of Abraham this oasis was a place people came to make up their spiritual minds. *En Mishpat* means "Spring of Decision."

God leads his people to this spring of decision. The decision at Kadesh has always involved the same questions: "Can I trust God?" "Do I really believe his promises?" Kadesh is a physical oasis where parched throats can be slaked. It is also a spiritual oasis where dehydrated faith can be revived. People pause at Kadesh to make up their minds about faith and trust. You either leave Kadesh as a person poised and pointed towards a promise or as a prisoner returning to the pits of the past.

Camped at Kadesh. Promised Land in view. Spies sent. Decision time.

Numbers 13:26-33 gives a fuller account:

> *They came back to Moses and Aaron and the whole Israelite community at Kadesh in the Desert of Paran. There they reported to them and to the whole assembly and showed them the fruit of the land. They gave Moses this account: "We went into the land to which you sent us, and it does flow with milk and honey! Here is its fruit. But the people who live there are powerful, and the cities are fortified and very large. We even saw descendants of Anak there. The Amalekites live in the Negev; the Hittites, Jebusites and Amorites live in the hill country; and the Canaanites live near the sea and along the Jordan. Then Caleb silenced the people before Moses and said, "We should go up and take possession of the land, for we can certainly do it."*
>
> *But the men who had gone up with him said, "We can't attack those people; they are stronger than we are." And they spread among the Israelites a bad report about the land they had explored. They said, "The land we explored devours those living in it. All the people we saw there are of great size. We saw the Nephilim there...*

> *we seemed like grasshoppers in our own eyes, and we looked the same to them.*

Kadesh. *The Spring of Decision*. Would these people leave this place as slaves or conquerors? Would they see opportunity or unsolvable challenges? Would they move towards deep change or would they opt for slow death, a return to slave mentality?

Slave thinking always focuses on the strength of the enemy more than the power of God.

Slave thinking always is more impressed with the chances for failure than it is with the opportunities for Godly victory.

Slave thinking will always be present in those who mentally have never left Egypt.

Slave thinking always spreads a bad report throughout the camp. "We seemed like grasshoppers in our own eyes, and we looked the same to them."

These people were on the edge of receiving all the promises God had made to their forefathers. Literally camped out at the border line of the Promised Land. But because they looked out at the challenges ahead through eyes of fear instead of faith, they were defeated without even facing the enemy!

SLAVISH DECISIONS

You can relate to Kadesh. You've spied out the options. You know where God wants you to be. But instead of stepping out in faith, you surrender in fear. Opportunities become obstacles too large to overcome. Fear drives your anxiety to a fevered pitch. The paranoid perceptions of the enslaved mind magnify imagined obstacles and erect walls of impossibility on the very blessing pathways of God. Its virus soon spreads to others in your camp.

And as slave thinking infects everyone the extent of the infection will shock you.

> *That night all the people of the community raised their voices and wept aloud. All the Israelites grumbled against Moses and Aaron, and the whole assembly said to them, "If only we had died in Egypt! Or in this desert! Why is the LORD bringing us to this land only to let us fall by the sword? Our wives and children will be taken as plunder. Wouldn't it be better for us to go back to Egypt?" And they said to each other, "We should choose a leader and go back to Egypt." (Numbers 14:1-4)*

From the summit of Sinai to the pinnacle of slave thinking! The people are completely unable to trust God's promises even after he demonstrated his love and power repeatedly. So what do they do? They start searching for a new leader. They look for someone that will take them back to Egypt!

You need to pay attention to their journey because yours can follow the same route. There's a place in your heart that you have hidden very well. A buried wound. A lost dream. A memory of unmet expectations or failure. A place where trust in God has not matured.

At that place slave thinking is still at work. Even now when doubt surfaces, when the faith walk gets increasingly difficult, when the challenge of discipleship confronts you, there is a place in all of us where we desire to go back. Even...back to Egypt. *Slow death is the devil we know, so we prefer it to the devil we do not know.*

As you tread on along the wilderness journey your hope may fade. Your vision may become blurred. The wilderness may be sucking your spirit dry. And you may be, at this very moment, longing to go back. Go back to whatever it is that is familiar. Go back to whatever it is you knew. But please listen. There is nothing for you back in Egypt. All you will find there is slavery. Slavery to sin that leads to death. It may be slow. But it is death. So come to Kadesh. Come thirsty and drink. Gulp a goblet of God's grace. Soak yourself in the fountain of his forgiveness. Look out through refreshed eyes at the promises he wants to give you. Stop for a moment under the palms of this place of soul searching and look long and hard at the two directions cast before you right now.

It's decision time. Will you follow him forward in faith or fall back in fear? But be forewarned. Your decision comes complete with consequences.

Decide for fear and furrow God's brow. The people want to reject the leader God has given them and go back to the place he delivered them from.

> *The LORD said to Moses, "How long will these people treat me with contempt? How long will they refuse to believe in me, in spite of all the miraculous signs I have performed among them?"* (Numbers 14:11)

God was ready to strike them down on the spot. But Moses, the leader the people would reject, interceded for them. And because the people preferred the wanderer mentality over the warrior, the slave mindset over the conqueror, God let them wander until all who had grumbled against him died out. Only Joshua and Caleb and the under twenty crowd would enjoy the land the others refused.

The people wished they had died in the desert. God told them they would get their wish. Can you imagine being an Israelite at that moment? They were literally standing on the brink of fulfilling a dream.

The dream began with Abraham.

Abraham passed the dream to Isaac.

Isaac passed the dream to Jacob.

Jacob passed the dream to his children.

The dream was passed to this very group. And they refused to receive it. At the spring of decision they decided to go back.

FAITH DECISIONS

And God decided to go forward. Without them. He will not force people to follow him. But he will forge ahead with those who will. Notice what he says to those who will survive the wilderness.

> *The* L*ORD said to Moses, "Speak to the Israelites and say to them: 'After you enter the land I am giving you as a home and you present to the* L*ORD offerings made by fire, from the herd or flock, as an aroma pleasing to the* L*ORD—whether burnt offerings or sacrifices....'" (Numbers 15:1-3)*

He takes those who believed they could enter the land and revives in them the dream. *"After you enter the land...."* Those with faith have always been the true descendants of Abraham. So God takes the dream and passes it on to those of faith. He prepares them over the next forty years to live with his presence.

The dream was entrusted to them because they made a decision for faith. They decided to look at every struggle, every moment of pain from the perspective of a warrior backed by the all powerful God rather than a wanderer without a home.

Don't you want to live with a faith like that?

What if you saw with the eyes of faith rather than fear? The wilderness of your life would look different. Every struggle, every moment of pain would be viewed from the perspective of a warrior instead of a slave. Wilderness would be seen as preparation for God's presence instead of something to simply endure.

Kadesh is decision time. It is time to believe the promises of God even before they become reality. Wilderness is not aimless adventure. Wilderness is not about punishment. Wilderness is about the transformation of your perspective towards a radical trust in the promises of God.

You are standing on the edge of promise. One foot in Egypt. One foot with God.

Decision time.

The next day Moses took his seat to serve as judge for the people, and they stood around him from morning till evening. When his father-in-law saw all that Moses was doing for the people, he said, "What is this you are doing for the people? Why do you alone sit as judge, while all these people stand around you from morning till evening?"

Moses answered him, "Because the people come to me to seek God's will. Whenever they have a dispute, it is brought to me, and I decide between the parties and inform them of God's decrees and laws."

EXODUS 18:13-16

Moses' father-in-law replied, "What you are doing is not good. You and these people who come to you will only wear yourselves out. The work is too heavy for you; you cannot handle it alone. Listen to me now and I will give you some advice, and may God be with you. You must be the people's representative before God and bring their disputes to him. Teach them the decrees and laws, and show them the way to live and the duties they are to perform."

EXODUS 18:17-20

FILE 12

HOW TO HANDLE LIFE OVERLOAD

EXODUS 18

Overload. 'owvurlowd' [v] fill to excess so that function is impaired.[1]

Mild-mannered drivers become raging road warriors because of it.

Blood pressures reach volcanic eruption levels as a result of it.

Nervous twitches surface as a symptom of it.

Overload.

Most Americans know the meaning. Their schedules are filled to excess and the result is impaired function. You can deposit the full impact of your blame into the Babylonian bank account. They failed to foresee the future of their overloaded descendants. (That would be us.) They divided the day into twenty-four hours. Experts tell us we need forty-one.[2]

Personal grooming. Men, 45 minutes. Women, 1 hour.

Cleaning teeth. 5 minutes.

Reading newspapers. 45 minutes.

Work. 8 hours.

Exercise. 1 hour.

"Quality time" with spouse. 15 minutes to 5 hours.

Pets. 2 hours.

Time with children. 4 hours, minimum. (Unless they are teenagers. In that case, 4 minutes, maximum, a day may be all you can stand.)

Leisure and sport. 2.6 hours.

Caring for others. 1.3 hours.

Internet. 3-5 hours.

Socializing. 41 minutes.

Reading. 22 minutes.
Sleep. 7.5 hours.

The rest of the time we need falls under other categories such as spiritual development, volunteering, watching TV, and making dinner. All take about one hour each. Add it up and you're in the forty-one hour a day ballpark.

Overload.

If your middle name is "overload" you probably want a quick solution. You could take the Red Queen's advice in *Alice in Wonderland* and try more motion. "Now here, you see, it takes all the running you can do, to keep in the same place. If you want to get somewhere else, you must run at least twice as fast as that!" Not much help is it? You've been there. Done that.

Overload.

Here's another option. Multi-task. Eat while you watch TV. Okay. Maybe better to exercise while you watch TV. Spend time with your kids while you volunteer. Shower with your dog. Or, listen to a book on tape while you eliminate things from your house. Not having spouses, kids, pets or plants would free up valuable hours.

If you don't like those options, try another suggestion. Move to Pluto. Pluto days last six times longer than an Earth day. Think of all the things you could do with six times the hours!

Instead of relocating or unloading, the real solution you are seeking may be found in changing the way you handle overload. Moses' plight will give you some pointers.

LEADER ON OVERLOAD

Moses was no stranger to overload. He had the responsibility of leading a nation of an estimated two million people. They are in the wilderness on their way to the Promised Land. He is their spiritual leader, a family man, and a judge for matters that come up between people. Two million of them.

When he meets up with his father-in-law Jethro he's been through the ringer. Back in chapter four Moses had left his wife, two sons and a request with Jethro. He had asked for permission to launch out on what had to be the most mind blowing, fantastic, presumptuous, cockamamie mission of all time. At eighty years of age Moses asked his father-in-law to bless his wild idea of going to the most powerful nation in the world and demanding that over a million people be set free.

If you're a father of a daughter, tell us, "What's Jethro thinking?!" He's used to being consulted about herd management issues. He's used to his brain being picked about defense strategies. He's used to his advice being sought for economic questions concerning the market. But this request? This one leaves him scratching his head.

The man who marries your daughter then turns around and leaves her and his kids with you to go off on a great adventure. The only thing more amazing is that he is now coming home with a whole nation in tow! And part of the deal of managing all of the people is overload.

Jethro is quick to recognize it. He saw Moses' drooping shoulders. The bags under his eyes. The endless wave of people coming to him 24/7.

> *The next day Moses took his seat to serve as judge for the people, and they stood around him from morning till evening. When his father-in-law saw all that Moses was doing for the people, he said, "What is this you are doing for the people? Why do you alone sit as judge, while all these people stand around you from morning till evening?"*
>
> *Moses answered him, "Because the people come to me to seek God's will. Whenever they have a dispute, it is brought to me, and I decide between the parties and inform them of God's decrees and laws." (Exodus 18:13-16)*

Want to become a warrior that is fighting the battles God wants you to fight? You won't become a warrior alone. And you won't be able to fight if you are lugging around overload.

Before he knew it, Moses had allowed a system to emerge that produced overload. First one pair of people in dispute came to Moses. Then another. And another. Before long it turned into a daily routine. Each day Moses would sit up and be sucked up into its vortex.

DANCING WITH OVERLOAD

We can get so addicted to the excess that function is impaired. One study showed that it takes a high dosage of amphetamines to kill a mouse living in solitude. Alone, a mouse can handle quite a bit. But a group of mice will hop around and excite each other so much that it takes a dosage "twenty times smaller" to be lethal. More revealing was the fact that a mouse not on drugs, placed in a group that was on the drug, will get so hopped up that within ten minutes it will die.[3]

We live in a world that is hopped up on the drug overload. It will pull you into its system. The first step out for Moses was *finding someone outside of the system to speak into his life.* And that's your first step too.

Jim Herrington of Mission Houston calls the "system pull" the "*dance.*" Moses appears to be part of a dance. His step was to take his seat. The people's step was to come to him and seek God's will. Moses was overloaded but nothing changed. The system kept things in place. The people kept coming. Moses kept listening. Nothing changed until he talked to Jethro.

Changing the dance is difficult. If you try, you tend to step on someone's toes. And that can be a painful experience. It's much easier to keep on dancing the old familiar dance steps.

So to change your dance steps you have to first stop dancing. Find a "dance instructor," someone you trust who knows you well. Ask that person to observe your dance and give you advice.

When you are on overload you are in some system that is impairing your function. It's a battle! One you can only win with the help of a "Jethro," and you can find yours by answering the following questions:

- If I have a concern about what is going in my faith community, who are the two or three people whom I would trust to go talk to about it?
- If I need insight or advice on a spiritual or church-related matter, whom do I go to?
- If I have a need that I believe the church can serve, whom do I go to?[4]

Just stepping outside of your system with your dance instructor will slow you down. And you have to slow down so you can learn new dance steps. It's similar to learning new runs on the guitar. Guitarists discover early that they have to slow down to speed up. They want to play fast and furious. But some notes and chord changes are difficult. The eyes don't pick up the movement quick enough and the fingers don't move fast enough.

To learn a new note or chord progression, it helps to slow down. Break a song down into smaller parts. Learn a section at a time. Slow down the changes until the hand-eye coordination is in place. Then you can handle more speed without feeling overloaded. Jethro interrupted the flow of people coming to Moses. It gave Moses a pause in his day to think and, with Jethro's help, discern his situation.

Warriors have to have breaks from the battle to get focused. Spiritual warriors do the same through solitude and silence. They schedule time to get away. They find ways to slow down. They experience Sabbath.

Jesus did. Sometimes he would slow down *after* an overloaded day by going away to lonely places (Mark 1:35). At other times he would go to the mountain *before* he went to the masses (Matthew 5:1). He knew the owner's manual and it reads, "Man shall not live at high RPM's for long."

When do you create "down time" in your schedule? To change your role in the system, part of your battle plan has to be some slowing down. Cut out an appointment. Curtail an activity. Collect your breath.

Here's what you will find: *life will go on*. You can pull away from the pressure and it will still be there when you get back. But *you* will be different. You will have had time to breathe again. You will have had time for spiritual reflection. You will have had time to create a new game plan. And you will have had time for God to dip his ladle into his well and give you a refreshing drink.

LEARNING YOUR DANCE STEPS

And while you are at a pause, *determine what is important for you to do.* Look at the wisdom Jethro shared with Moses.

> *Moses' father-in-law replied, "What you are doing is not good. You and these people who come to you will only wear yourselves out. The work is too heavy for you; you cannot handle it alone. Listen to me now and I will give you some advice, and may God be with you. You must be the people's representative before God and bring their disputes to him. Teach them the decrees and laws, and show them the way to live and the duties they are to perform." (Exodus 18:17-20)*

Here's a father-in-law who knew how to speak the truth. What was happening was not good—for anybody involved.

But notice what Jethro did not say. He didn't tell Moses to walk away. He didn't tell Moses to take a vacation. There were things Moses was called to do.

He was called to represent the people before God.

He was called to teach them and show them the way to live.

The problem was he was caught up in activity that he was not meant to be doing. No one had told him he was not to sit and hear every single dispute day after day. Until Jethro.

Warriors know what it is they are to do. Commanders plan. Generals lead. Soldiers fight. And they don't get caught up in "civilian" matters

(2 Timothy 2:4). Gary Thomas says, "We have to realize we don't need to know all that we want to know; we need to cultivate the discipline of letting go of cares that don t concern us."[5]

You don't have to know everything or give your opinion on everything—or even *have* an opinion on everything.

Thomas says that it would be entirely justifiable for a basketball coach to give a stern rebuke to a player who showed up tired for a night game because he had run a marathon earlier that morning. Likewise, a boss would not accept an excuse from a worker who showed up exhausted because she stayed up watching television all night. He says, "Coaches and bosses expect us to conserve our energy for what really matters. God expects no less."[6]

God has given you a mission. One way to escape overload is to review the mission. Make a list of the activities that have crowded your schedule. For each activity ask yourself, "How does this activity help advance the mission?"

You may chuckle at some. "How does a shower fit in?" The answer is obvious, "Love your neighbor." But others may cause you to choke. Endless meetings. Hours of television. Even a full calendar of church activities. Your Jethro or group of Jethros can help you here. Let them ask you the tough questions.

God is shaping you into a warrior, someone ready for battle. Jesus defined the battle as "going, making disciples of all nations, teaching and baptizing" (Matthew 28:19-20). Do you find any of that on your list? Be honest. If not, why not?

Perhaps we are more like Moses than we thought. Doing things that look good but, as Jethro says, "are not good." Something has to change. And that's the last step in getting a handle on overload. *Start behaving in new ways*. Here's what you've done so far.

You've pulled away from the dance and sought advice from someone outside of the system.

You've created some space so you can slow down in order to speed up.

You've been reminded of what it is you are supposed to do.

And when you go back into the dance...you'll want to dance the same way you did before. It's easy. It's comfortable. But you have to change the dance.

Jethro helped Moses learn some new dance steps. Yes, people needed help with their problems. But Moses did not have to take care of everyone. Jethro pointed him to a better way of dancing.

> *But select capable men from all the people—men who fear God, trustworthy men who hate dishonest gain—and appoint them as officials over thousands, hundreds, fifties and tens. Have them serve as judges for the people at all times, but have them bring every difficult case to you; the simple cases they can decide themselves. That will make your load lighter, because they will share it with you. If you do this and God so commands, you will be able to stand the strain, and all these people will go home satisfied. Moses listened to his father-in-law and did everything he said. (Exodus 18:21-24)*

It's probably the most difficult verse in the Bible to believe, but "Moses listened to his father-in-law and did everything he said." (Some scholars— Rick and Reg—believe that Jethro inserted that line when Moses wasn't looking.)

It took some effort. It took some teaching and modeling. Chances are that Moses was tempted to jump in and take on some of the more simple cases. But the dance did change.

And because it did we can imagine things turned out just as Jethro said they would. The people went home satisfied. Moses went home with less of a load. And Jethro? He just went home. "Then Moses sent his father-in-law on his way, and Jethro returned to his own country" (Exodus 18:27).

Feeling a bit overloaded? Then join Moses on the dance floor.

Your only other option may be to move to Pluto.

Remember the Sabbath day by keeping it holy. Six days you shall labor and do all your work, but the seventh day is a Sabbath to the LORD your God. On it you shall not do any work, neither you, nor your son or daughter, nor your manservant or maidservant, nor your animals, nor the alien within your gates. For in six days the LORD made the heavens and the earth, the sea, and all that is in them, but he rested on the seventh day. Therefore the LORD blessed the Sabbath and made it holy.

EXODUS 20:8-11

FILE 13

DAY PLANNERS, BIG ROCKS AND PARTIES

EXODUS 12; 20:8-11; 23; 30; 34; LEVITICUS 23:23-25

You decide this is the year you will finally get organized. Out comes the calendar. A cafeteria line of events is spread in front of you from which to choose. But you're like a deer caught in the headlights on where to begin.

A story comes to mind about a seminar presenter who placed a wide mouth gallon jar on the stage. He filled it to the top with some big rocks. He asked the audience if it was full and they yelled back, "Yes!"

The presenter then took some smaller, gravelly rocks and poured them into the container. He asked again, "Is the jar full?" Catching on, the people said, "Probably not." Next went in sand followed by water until the jar was absolutely saturated.

One participant missed the point. He said, "You can always put more things on your schedule if you really work at it." The presenter countered, "No, if you don't put the big rocks in first you would never get the rest of them in."[1]

You come back to your calendar and start marking the "big rocks": *Birthdays. Baby Showers. Baseball games. Holidays. Vacations. Anniversary.*

You get the point. Families, companies, even churches pull out the calendar and mark the most significant dates first. If some events are missed, husbands wind up on the couch. If others are missed, momentous moments can be forgotten.

Maybe that's why God did an unusual thing with Moses. He had him pull out his *Day-Planner* and mark down some dates. Dates when these wanderers-turned-warriors would stop and party. God showed Moses which rocks to put in first.

RHYTHM OF REMEMBRANCE

He started with the Sabbath. Fifty-two times a year, once each week, the people were to stop.

> *Remember the Sabbath day by keeping it holy. Six days you shall labor and do all your work, but the seventh day is a Sabbath to the LORD your God. On it you shall not do any work, neither you, nor your son or daughter, nor your manservant or maidservant, nor your animals, nor the alien within your gates. For in six days the LORD made the heavens and the earth, the sea, and all that is in them, but he rested on the seventh day. Therefore the LORD blessed the Sabbath and made it holy. (Exodus 20:8-11)*

Every week the calendar said *stop*.

Every week the calendar said *rest*.

Every week the calendar said *remember*. Remember what is important. Remember your focus. Remember your God.

Why so much remembering? God wants his people to remember because people tend to forget what is important. We get caught up in the duties and the deadlines and the disappointments. And we forget.

But God doesn't. The rhythm of remembrance is found in creation. For six days God created. Each day he said, "It is good." Then he looked at what the work of his hands had accomplished and remembered, "It is very good."

A day to remember was so good God blessed it. He starts Moses' *Day-Planner* off with a time to stop and remember each week because he knew that if his people lived their weeks right they would live their years right. And if they lived their years right they would live their lives right.

So he asked them to claim a day each week so that they could reclaim their faith each week. In doing so they developed a habit of remembering.

And they would need it. The pattern of his people would be to forget what he had done for them. So God takes his loom and begins weaving into their lives threads of colorful events to help them remember. After Moses marked down fifty-two weekly days to remember, God had him put in five annual big rocks.

RESCUE

Each year they would remember their rescue from slavery in the *Feast of the Passover* (Exodus 12; Leviticus 23:4-8). They would remember a desperate night when they waited for God to act. Slaves in Egypt for four hundred years, they had been witnesses to nine devastating plagues that had not convinced Pharaoh to free them. Something more would be necessary. Their freedom would come at a great price.

And so they waited. They ate. They packed. They marked their doorposts. Then God acted just as he said he would. Their rescue from slavery was bought with the lives of firstborn sons across Egypt—including Pharaoh's. It was an event that had to be memorialized.

God gave Moses the blueprint for the memorial the very night the people were freed by his hand. Talk about big rocks! Remembering their rescue was so significant it literally procured first page position on the calendar.

> *This month is to be...the first month of your year....This is a day you are to commemorate; for the generations to come you shall celebrate it as a festival to the Lord—a lasting ordinance. (Exodus 12:2, 14)*

Each year God's people set aside seven days to remember their rescue by throwing a big festival with food, family, and stories that all reenacted the Passover. All so their rescue would be remembered.

RENEWED LOVE

Fifty days later celebration would start up again. Just enough time would pass to recover from the Passover celebration when another one would get underway. *Pentecost* (Exodus 34:22; Leviticus 23:15-17). Sometimes called the Feast of Weeks, this rock remembered the renewal of God's covenant love.

Everyone in the land would stop working again. (You're starting to like this calendar, aren't you?) They would hold the very grain that would keep them alive for another year, the first fruits. They would thank God for what he had given them. And they would remember. They would remember how much God loved them with his covenant of love.

Pentecost was initiated at another landmark moment in the history of Israel when the people were camped at the foot of God's mountain. The LORD had spoken the Ten Words. Moses had received from God the invitation to eternal covenant love written on stone.

But when Moses made it down the mountain, he met the Israelites in the midst of an orgy! In anger he smashed the tablets of stone to the ground. Imagine the fear in the hearts of the people as they came to their senses. They had seen the thunder and lightning, smelled the smoke and heard the trumpet. What would God do with them?

It was at this very point that he marked Pentecost on the calendar. Having caught his people in the middle of their unfaithfulness, God did the unexpected. He renewed his love for them.

A renewed love is a deeper form of love. Picture for a moment a common scenario. A man and woman stand before the preacher and exchange vows. They're young. They're in love. And they're clueless. They have a love, but it is not a love that has been tried. They don't know the faults and foibles of the other.

But move the story ahead twenty-five years. They renew their love for each other by renewing their vows. And somehow the words "for better or worse" carry with them a deeper meaning. Once, they chose each other before the faults. Now, they choose each other again in spite of them.

They remember and renew. God did the same for the Israelites. He renewed his love for his people and marked it on the calendar. He did the same for you. "While we were still sinners, Christ died for us" (Romans 5:8). God wants his people to remember his desire to live in their midst.

RELOCATION

And he did live in their midst in the Tabernacle. Which may be the most abnormal annual event scheduled on the calendar. So that they would remember their days of wandering the people would relocate once a year. They marked it as the *Feast of Tabernacles* (Exodus 23:16; Exodus 34; Leviticus 23:33-43).

Imagine the scene. All of Israel would build little booths or huts out of branches. Then they would live in these temporary shelters for seven days. During this time they would remember when they or their ancestors lived in tents in the wilderness. They would recall their longing for a home and how God relocated them from Egypt to the Promised Land.

RANSOM

The Feast of Tabernacles followed right after the *Day of Atonement* festival (Exodus 30:10; Leviticus 16; 23:26-32). This festival ushered in both good and bad news for the people. The good news? They got to take a break from work again. The bad news? They took a break from eating too. This was the only commanded fast on the calendar.

The people would take all their attention normally given to work and food and redirect it towards the ransom made for their lives. They watched as the priest entered the Holy of Holies in the temple and sent all of the guilt of God's people back to Satan. That's something to blow your horn about.

REVOLUTION

And that's what they did. What kicked off this entire seventh month was the *Feast of the Trumpets* (Leviticus 23:23-25). This feast lasted only one day, but it was a blast. It was a day of Sabbath rest that began with the sounding of long, loud trumpets.

Imagine the sound of dozens of shofars—ram's horn trumpets emitting a low bold blast—echoing across the stone walled city. Old warriors suddenly rise remembering that sound from by-gone days of life and death battle. Young men stop, eyes glistening, fixed on the sound that carries with it the stories of heritage and a national inheritance built upon a fearless faith. Over and over again fathers answer the questions of children by passing on a testimony and witness to the wonder of following God.

The trumpet blast reminded them of the traditional call to war—to leave the wandering life behind and become warriors.

Picture the sequence. The seventh month rolls around and you wake up to an hour of trumpet blasts. Nine days later you and your family stop and spend a focused day on the fact that your sins are forgiven. Five days later you pack up the family and move to a temporary tabernacle in the yard. You live there for a week, book-ending it with burnt offerings.

God had Moses pull out the *Day Planner* and put the big dates in first.

REVOLUTIONIZE YOUR LIFE

Now, imagine for a moment what it was like to have a life shaped by remembrance, by seasons of celebration and thanksgiving. It may be difficult to do so because we live in a culture where we look forward to vacation time. The ancient person of faith would look forward to days dedicated to thanking God for what he had done in his life. It was a vastly different way to live. All of life was framed by a priceless cycle of remembering and celebrating God. And we have lost it.

But what is lost can be found. Envision what it would be like for your life to be shaped by remembrance. Stopping is your first step. Create a Sabbath in your week. One day where you turn off the TV. Turn off the computer. Turn off the world. Surround yourself with family and friends. Feast together. Remember the good in God's creation. And be thankful. How much would your life be altered if you developed the habit of fifty-two Thanksgiving Days a year?

Your stress would be less and your faith would grow. Before you could be diverted off center you would find your north star and stay on course.

And what if every couple of months you added other celebrations? Your initial response may be "there's no way!"

> According to a recent Expedia.com study on U.S. vacation habits, Americans were allowed an average of 16 vacation days in 2002, but most only took 14 days off, handing back more than $21 billion in unused vacation days to their employers. In most European nations, by contrast, an average of about 30 vacation days is the norm, and so are shorter work weeks.[2]

Your cultural conditioning may not lead to celebrating. But following God should. And not just any celebrating. You have the usual friends, family, food, and festivities. But he adds a new twist. He adds the remembrance.

So come into the war room with us for a moment. Bring your *Day-Planner* with you. And ask, "What if?"

What if once a year you planned time off to remember your rescue? You quietly contemplate how God rescued you from the dominion of darkness and brought you into the kingdom of the Son he loves (Colossians 1:13)?

What if once a year you took time off and renewed your vows to God? Maybe you do this on the date of your baptism. Or maybe a time you remember making solid promises to God. Once again you confess with your mouth that Jesus is your Lord (Romans 10:9). Others hear it. Friends know it.

That even after years of journeying through wilderness and wars, you confess that the God who knows the depths of your heart still loves you. And you love him.

What if once a year you relocated? Not literally *relocate*. But what if you took a trip to a temporary shelter? A place by the beach. A cabin in the mountains. A Days Inn downtown. Somewhere other than your home where you can remember what is it like to be away from home. You meditate on the truth that God has taken you as an orphan and adopted you into his family (Romans 8:15; Ephesians 1:5). You stay in an unfamiliar bed long enough to dream of the one back home. And you understand more clearly that you are an alien in a world that is not your home (1 Peter 1:11).

What if once a year you set aside a few days to remember the ransom paid for your sin? You reflect on the cross. You see the crown. You hear the hammer. You feel the nails. You hear the cry. You read again how Jesus entered the Holy of Holies after paying the price for your guilt (Hebrews 9:11-14).

This is no momentary remembrance. This is a time to listen. This is a time to learn. This is a time to linger at the cross for the full impact of the price that was paid for your ransom. Remember that you were captured by the enemy. Recall your savior tearing down the very gates of hell to deliver the payment for your life with his own.

Do you think that might be *revolutionary*?

Your life would be marked by remembrance of the significant moments in your life with God.

Your life would be marked by a holy intimacy with God.

Your life would be marked by a confidence that your sins are forgiven.

And your life would be marked by thanksgiving. Always thanking God for salvation, for victory, for life itself. You would see that one who was once a wanderer was being transformed into a warrior.

What if you turned your gaze towards God on a regular basis? Along with more holidays, you might find more holy days.

So remember. Put the big rocks in the jar first.

"Then have them make a sanctuary for me, and I will dwell among them. Make this tabernacle and all its furnishings exactly like the pattern I will show you.

Have them make a chest of acacia wood—two and a half cubits long, a cubit and a half wide, and a cubit and a half high. Overlay it with pure gold, both inside and out, and make a gold molding around it. Cast four gold rings for it and fasten them to its four feet, with two rings on one side and two rings on the other. Then make poles of acacia wood and overlay them with gold. Insert the poles into the rings on the sides of the chest to carry it. The poles are to remain in the rings of this ark; they are not to be removed."

EXODUS 25:8-15

FILE 14

THE TENT STAKE PEOPLE

EXODUS 25:8-9, 15

According to *American Demographics*,[1] the older Americans get the more they like to put down stakes. Only one-tenth of people aged forty-five and older move to a new address each year. In contrast, trends throughout the nineties indicated that one-third of people in their twenties change their addresses every year. Young adults are the largest segment in our society who are on the move. Factor into the equation that eighty percent of movers are renters and it's a simple calculation: it is much easier to move when you haven't put your stakes down too deep or for too long.

Overall, Americans are moving less than they used to. After the age of thirty the likelihood of moving declines steadily. The older we get the more we like to put down stakes and stay put. People tend to resist movement.

This tendency is nothing new. The Israelites resisted movement too. It didn't take long for them to be in the wilderness before they were crying to go back to Egypt. They were slaves there but at least there they knew where their next meal was coming from and they had a roof over their heads.

Maybe that was part of their problem. They were accustomed to living in the ways of the Egyptians rather than the ways of God. The only life they had known for hundreds of years consisted of working like a slave during the day and coming home to the same house each night. God eventually let all the grumblers die off until all that were left were those who had grown up in the wilderness way of life. This new generation was used to moving.

IN THE MOVING BUSINESS

God is young at heart when it comes to changing addresses. Like the renter, he is prone to move. He took a multitude of people who had one address for four hundred years, moved them into a wilderness, and relocated them to Mt. Sinai. U-Haul would have made a killing off this caravan of travelers.

Once they reached Mt. Sinai they might have thought their journey was over. In those days it was believed that gods resided on mountains, far away from immediate contact with the people. It is on a mountain, however, that they discovered our God is different.

Moses took the commandments in stride.

No other gods. Check.

No idols. Check.

No misuse of my name. Check.

Then something out of left field. "Make a tent for me and I will dwell among you" (Exodus 25:8).

Moses realized God was not going to settle on the summit of Mt. Sinai. God is a God on the move. And notice what else he tells Moses. "Moses, make me an ark. No, not as big as the one Noah made. This one will have gold rings. Two on each side. Put some poles through those rings. But don't take the poles out. Leave them in the rings" (Exodus 25:10-16).

Why were the poles left in the rings?

The same reason you and I keep our car keys handy.

The same reason firefighters live at the fire station.

The same reason Spiderman wears his Spidey-suit under his clothes.

When it is time to move there is no time to waste. That's why God chose to dwell among the people in a tabernacle. Tabernacles, or "tents," are made for movement. "Gods" who value a sedentary life do not inhabit tabernacles. "Gods" who wish to remain remote do not request a tent.

Tabernacles are for a God who is on the move. Tabernacles are for a God who is committed to intimacy with the people.

"Why the Tabernacle?" We're glad you asked. When you go camping you don't take your house along with you, do you? It would be too large, too bulky to bundle in your backpack. Instead you take a tent. You can move from campsite to campsite, wherever the spirit leads you.

And that is exactly what God wants his people to learn. He wants us to be ready to move with him whenever the Spirit leads.

That's why Jesus came and lived among us. When John wrote the words of John 1:14, the word he used for "lived" among us is literally "tabernacled" among us. John says of Jesus: "He pitched his tent among us." Like Father, like Son.

THE HIGH STAKES OF MOVING

Now notice what is at stake in this revelation about God. God made his dwelling among the Israelite people. His tent was in the middle of their tents. It was portable and ready to move. Each morning and each night the people would watch. If the cloud by day or the column of fire by night were to shift, everyone packed up and moved.

Imagine what would happen if someone in the group decided they did not want to go. Over in tent # 6,483 Benjamin and Beulah are retiring for the night. Old Ben is in his pajamas, half-asleep. Beulah—hair rolled up in curlers—peeks out from their tent one last time.

"Ben, wake up! The column of fire is moving again!"

"Oh, Beulah. Would you settle down! I just fell asleep. Let's wait till in the morning and we'll catch up."

"Ben, you know we can't do that. We're in the wilderness."

"Yeah? What difference does it make?"

"I'll tell you what difference it makes. We'll be at the mercy of the wild beasts. Or an army could attack us. There's safety in numbers, you know."

"Well, I'll take my chances. Anything else you want to say before I go back to sleep? I was dreaming that we were eating something other than frosted flakes for breakfast."

"I can think of one last thing. If we don't go, we won't be with God."

When God moved, a lot was riding on the Israelites' response. Safety. Security. Sustenance. But the main issue at stake was that the people would be missing out on the movement of God.

The same is true today. When God moves, will we be content to let him move on while we sleep in? Will we let him find others who will follow while we dig our stakes in a little deeper? What is at stake with us is what was at stake for the Israelites. If we do not move with God, we will miss out on his movement.

We have a choice. Either pull up stakes and move with God or put down stakes and be left without God.

MOVING RESPONSES

In the Gospel accounts we learn that while Jesus pitched his tent among us he was amazed in one of two ways.

Jesus was amazed by lack of movement in response to him. Mark records a time when Jesus was the scandal of his hometown. They could not believe that he was who he claimed to be. And Jesus could do no great work of power there. Why? Because he was "amazed at their unbelief" (Mark 6:6).

Jesus was also amazed by great faith. For example, consider the story of the Canaanite woman. She came to Jesus and started shouting, "Have mercy on me, Lord, Son of David; my daughter is tormented by a demon" (Matthew 15:21ff.). Notice she does not seem to mind causing a scene. And she doesn't mind if everyone in earshot knows her daughter has a demon. (Our guess is the others had teenage daughters too.)

The disciples get embarrassed and try to send her away. Jesus tries to test her mettle. He reminds her that he has come to the household of Israel. She asks again for help. He tells her it isn't right to take food for children and throw it to the dogs. But she's a persistent pup. She reminds him that even dogs are satisfied with the crumbs. "Woman, great is your faith!" Jesus says,

"Let it be done to you as you wish." Jesus gets excited. The woman gets her daughter back minus the demon.

God's concern when he pitched his tent in the wilderness is the same as Jesus' concern when he pitched his tent among us. He wants to see his people move when he moves. God is drawn to motion and activity that comes in response to his leading. And he will be amazed by one of two things: our lack of faith or our evidence of faith.

God desires his people to move even today. And yet the average Christian looks little different from his or her non-Christian neighbor. God wants to pitch his tent among us and lead us to a new way of life. When we sense his movement we can respond in one of two ways.

We can put our stakes down deeper and refuse to follow because the future is not clear. We can let the fear of the unknown cause us to become settlers instead of sojourners.

Or...we can pull up stakes and move with God! Satan cannot bear to hear tent stakes being pulled up all around the camp. He will do whatever he can to make us put them right back in the ground. He will make us queasy with his questions: "Do you know where God's path will lead you? Do you know each step of the way?"

And of course, the answer to both questions is "No!" If we knew we would not have to exercise the muscles of faith. Faith is trust. And trust is not built by roadmaps and directional signals. Faith is built by relational experience with God. If you know the way, you don't need God. But when you are in the wilderness you won't dare take a step without him.

Our physical lives tend to mirror our spiritual lives. When we are young in age, we rent. We keep ourselves free to move. We love the adventure. As we get older, we become more sedentary. We set our stakes and stay put.

When we are young in spirit, we are ready to follow wherever God leads. But as we get older we lose our desire to follow. We want things settled. We want to know all the answers. We think we know the way ourselves. There is enough chaos in our lives that we don't want God to lead us on an adventure.

FAITH MOVEMENTS

The truth is if we walk only on paths where we know each step of the way, then we do not walk by faith. We don't need God's guidance. And so we stop listening. We stop obeying. We quit looking to him every day and every night to see if the cloud or fire is moving.

We focus on our own road maps. We lean on our own understanding. And we put down stakes and curl up on the couch.

Maybe it is time for God's people to pray that he will land us in the wilderness so that we have no secure fixed place to call home. A wilderness where the old maps of "how things have always been done" don't work anymore. A land where new maps are needed.

The God who chose a tent and the Jesus who called out "follow" have not changed. Their desire is for us to learn to trust. Learn to have faith. Learn to live by taking steps of faith.

Faith breeds on movement.

Following God into the unknown as the Israelites did opens us up to the dynamic of growing faith. It takes very little faith to remain in the same place spiritually and never move. But to move out with God into the unknown takes radical faith.

So when the future is unclear...

When all the questions can't be answered...

When fear wants to freeze you...

...hear the call. "Pull up the stakes. Let's move. Follow me!"

Look for God in the movement. Find someone with a tent stake dangling out of their back pocket and get in line.

You don't want to get left behind.

Then we turned back and set out toward the desert along the route to the Red Sea, as the LORD had directed me. For a long time we made our way around the hill country of Seir. Then the LORD said to me, "You have made your way around this hill country long enough; now turn north."

DEUTERONOMY 2:1

Thirty-eight years passed from the time we left Kadesh Barnea until we crossed the Zered Valley. By then, that entire generation of fighting men had perished from the camp, as the LORD had sworn to them.

DEUTERONOMY 2:14

FILE 15

WARRIORS IN THE LAND

EXODUS 24:15-27:21; NUMBERS 21

Imagine baking the Thanksgiving turkey. You cram it with stuffing. Season the gravy to perfection. Prepare the pumpkin pie. Set the table with your holiday finest. Sit down with a house full of relatives and friends...

...and never feast on it.

Picture going to the Christmas tree farm. Your family picks out the perfect pine. With the skill of a Clark Griswald you strap it to the top of your car. With great struggle you force it through the front door. Pinball it through the hallway to its privileged position. Set it up in its stand. String it up in its lights. Add ornaments. Pile presents around the base...

...and never open any of them.

Envision being the owner of a sweepstakes ticket. The winning number is announced. A financial windfall is yours. Your sole responsibility is to report with ticket in hand to a certified station. You drive to the address. You get out of your car. In a few steps a life of luxury will be within your grasp. You walk up to the door...

...and keep walking in circles around the block.

Sounds irrational, doesn't it? Who would come so close to the feast you could almost taste it...and not taste it? Who would look the gift horse in the mouth...and not take the gift? Who would be within a step of securing a lifestyle of the rich and famous...and not take the step?

HOVERING AROUND HORMAH

Hard to believe, but it happened. It happened at a place called Kadesh Barnea. You'll remember that it was the oasis on the edge of the Promised Land. It was the promise of a Thanksgiving feast, a truckload of Christmas presents, and a winning ticket wrapped up in one location.

But instead of Kadesh becoming the place where the people of Israel claimed what God was setting before them, they let Kadesh become the launching pad for four decades of wilderness wandering. They doubted God would give them the land. So they did not feast on what was before them. They did not open gifts that were promised to them. They did not receive the payload that was theirs.

Oh, they had some second thoughts, mind you. They cooked up a plan of their own to take the land in their own power without God's blessing. And that recipe always leads to disaster.

> *"We have sinned," they said. "We will go up to the place the LORD promised."*
>
> *But Moses said, "Why are you disobeying the LORD's command? This will not succeed! Do not go up, because the LORD is not with you. You will be defeated by your enemies, for the Amalekites and Canannites will face you there. Because you have turned away from the LORD, he will not be with you and you will fall by the sword."*
>
> *Nevertheless, in their presumption they went up toward the high hill country, though neither Moses nor the ark of the LORD's covenant moved from the camp. Then the Amalekites and Canaanites who lived in that hill country came down and attacked them and beat them down all the way to Hormah. (Numbers 14:40-45)*

Hormah is located at the south end of the Promised Land. On the edge but not over. Almost there but not quite.

Hormah is a single Hebrew word with a double meaning. It can mean "doom." It can also mean "devoted to God." It can carry with it the sense of destruction when you completely destroy something because you offer it as a sacrifice.

But for the Israelites who tried to take matters into their own hands and leave God out, Hormah spelled "doom." The city sign read "Doomsville." The Israelites felt the full impact of its etymology. They were doomed to almost drop off the map. After this defeat there is little information on what happens to this group for the next thirty-eight years.[1] One verse in Deuteronomy chronicles forty years of wandering.

> *Then we turned back and set out toward the desert along the route to the Red Sea, as the LORD had directed me. For a long time we made our way around the hill country of Seir. Then the LORD said to me, "You have made your way around this hill country long enough; now turn north." (Deuteronomy 2:1)*

A few verses later the author records these words:

> *Thirty-eight years passed from the time we left Kadesh Barnea until we crossed the Zered Valley. By then, that entire generation of fighting men had perished from the camp, as the LORD had sworn to them. (Deuteronomy 2:14)*

Read between the lines and you hear an amazing absurdity. During the four decades of wandering these people never strayed more than a few days' walk from the Promised Land. For four decades they hovered next to a land they could not enter because they had a trust problem.

Though they had left the slave yards of Egypt they were still enslaved in their minds. God sent them into a cycle of circling in the wilderness to bring them to a breakthrough in their thinking. Before they could cross over into a new land they would have to cross over into a new spiritual perspective. Struggle would be the classroom of transformation.

Climbers understand. No climber has reaped the rewards of the mountain without making an agreement with suffering. Suffering and struggle are accepted parts of life to the climber. Who else would eat trail mix when not on the trail? Who else would choose to go outside with a small shovel instead of staying inside and making use of modern conveniences? Who else chooses to put up with cold rain instead of staying in the comfort and warmth of a rain proof home? Who else but backpackers sit at work dreaming of the next time they can go suffer some more?

Somewhere on the trail the climber learns to look past the pain. And somewhere in the wilderness God's people learn the same. They listen for the time God says, "You have been going in circles long enough."

Finally he tells the Israelites to turn north.

TURNING INTO WARRIORS

When they do they face their first big challenge after four decades of wandering. "When the Canaanite king of Arad...heard that Israel was coming along the road to Atharim, he attacked the Israelites and captured some of them" (Numbers 21:1).

For the first time in four decades they prepare to end the circling and move towards the Promised Land. God has been preparing them in the harshest of conditions. The Negev is no vacation spot. 127 degrees on a cool day. They've told and retold the stories about some spies who reported they would be like grasshoppers to the inhabitants of the land.

But those spies are dead now. And buried with them was their old perspective and vision. So the post-wilderness Israelites enter their first conflict. And boom! They experience a huge setback: *he* [the Canaanite king of Arad] *attacked the Israelites and captured some of them*. Promised Land? Milk and honey? More like a *Smack Down* event with the first enemy they face. You know someone had to be looking at this situation and saying to themselves, "Maybe the spies were right." What will their next move be?

38 years earlier they would have started sprinting back to Egypt.

38 years earlier they would have burned Moses at the stake.

38 years earlier they would have looked at every struggle from the perspective of a slave victim mentality.

But that was 38 years earlier. They've experienced the wilderness. They've experienced faith training. They've experienced God. This time they look squarely into the face of pain and petition God for power. "Then Israel made this vow to the LORD: 'If you deliver these people into our hands, we will totally destroy their cities'" (Numbers 21:2).

Something has changed. And it isn't their circumstances. The people see things from a radically new perspective. Oh, they are still an unruly band of whiners. But they are unruly whiners who now see the world through the eyes of free men instead of slaves.

They have been fashioned into fierce warriors.

They have been trained to trust God.

They have been transformed from house maids and spineless brick layers into a serious attack army of God!

And that's how they behave. They vow to devote the battle completely to God. They vow to utterly destroy the enemy and everything they touch. This means they will annihilate all booty as a sacrifice to God. Everything is dedicated to the LORD.

DISCIPLINED CHANGE

What changed their mindset? The struggle of the wilderness.

Climbers understand. So do God's people. There is a transformation that only comes through a love that disciplines.

And you have forgotten that word of encouragement that addresses you as sons: "My son, do not make light of the Lord's discipline, and do not lose heart when he rebukes you because the Lord disciplines those he loves, and he punishes everyone he accepts as a son." Endure hardship as discipline; God is treating you as sons. For what son is not disciplined by his father? If you are not disciplined (and everyone undergoes discipline) then you are illegitimate children and not true sons. Moreover, we have all had human fathers who disciplined us and we respected them for it. How much more should we submit to the Father of our spirits and live! Our fathers disciplined us for a little while as they thought best; but God disciplines us for our good, that we may share in his holiness. No discipline seems pleasant at the time, but painful. Later on, however, it produces a harvest of righteousness and peace for those who have been trained by it. (Hebrews 12:5-11)

God's discipline in the wilderness produced a harvest. Slave thinking was buried and a conqueror mindset was raised. The first indication of this radically new perspective is seen in how the people handle defeat. The chains of victim mentality are broken. They have a radically new perspective about themselves, about their circumstances, and about God.

The second indication of change is seen in how they handle victory. They display a radical obedience. "The LORD listened to Israel's plea and gave the Canaanites over to them. They completely destroyed them and their towns; so the place was named Hormah" (Numbers 21:3).

Hormah. Same place you've been before. Same circumstance as before. But something is different. The people have changed.

38 years earlier Hormah was a place of defeat. Now it has become the place of victory.

38 years earlier it was a place of doom. Now it is a place of complete devotion to God.

38 years earlier it was a place where the people began wandering. Now it is the place where the people become warriors.

38 years earlier it was a place of judgment against a generation. Now it is the place of judgment against all enemies of God.

The difference is all about perspective and obedience. The people have a radically new outlook on the events of their lives. And the people are ready to radically obey God.

They interpret everything that happens to them through the lens of God's power, provision, and providence. They change the sign from "Doom" to "Devoted." They see the feast and eat. They hold the presents and open. They take the ticket and receive.

They enter the land of promise.

And to their surprise they find the land of promise is not a geographical location. The land of promise is found in the heart.

The wandering. The waiting. The imprint on their lives. The life map. The struggle with systems that enslaved them. The internal battle between fear and faith. The spring of decision. All places that had more to do with their heart than with a homeland. More to do with their spirit than a mere spot.

IT'S YOUR TURN

And you've journeyed with them. The same wandering and waiting. The same struggle and battles. The same decisions. Maybe you too have discovered there is a place in the heart where faith works miracles. Faith brings you home wherever you are because wherever you are you are home with God.

Through the eyes of faith you have found a place where the trials of life are somehow transformed into blessing. You have come to the place that exists in the soul of every offspring of Abraham where vision is derived not from what the eye can see but from what the heart understands.

You have crossed over into the land where you finally walk by faith and not sight.

Struggle no longer sends you packing. Suffering does not stop you in your steps. You do not feel what everyone else feels. You do not see things the way everyone else sees. You have been transformed to have the heart and eyes of faith.

Just like another ancestor of Abraham who arrived there ahead of us. The apostle Paul. His words are the words of a backpacker that has made peace with suffering.

> *But we have this treasure in jars of clay to show that this all-surpassing power is from God and not from us. We are hard pressed on every side, but not crushed; perplexed, but not in despair; persecuted, but not abandoned; struck down, but not destroyed. We always carry around in our body the death of Jesus, so that the life of Jesus may also be revealed in our body. (2 Corinthians 4:7-10)*

Paul had a radically different perspective. He looked past the pain and saw the provision. He understood that suffering was a part of the package. But struggle was the only place he could go to learn a trust beyond the fake reality that swirled around him. Jeremy Camp captures Paul's sentiments in his song *Walk by Faith*.

I will walk by faith
Even when I cannot see
Because this broken road
Prepares your will for me.[2]

The "broken roads" of graveyards, caskets, tombstones and funerals did not have the final say in the meaning of Paul's life. It doesn't have to have the final say in yours. Your reality is not dictated by the weakness of your flesh. The things that overwhelm you do not have to define you.

But they can prepare you for God's will for you. There is a treasure in the jar of clay that is you. Paul says the suffering brings him to a place where he has something to give. A revelation in his body of the life of Jesus.

Don't miss this! There is a glory that wants to be revealed in the broken places of your life. No longer do you have to be a member of the church of secrets. Instead of living in hiddenness, you can live in a loving, repenting, forgiving community of grace and truth. And through the brokenness of your life the radiance of God's glory will shine.

Paul maps out the journey this way:

> *Therefore we do not lose heart. Though outwardly we are wasting away, yet inwardly we are being renewed day by day. For our light and momentary troubles are achieving for us an eternal glory that far outweighs them all. So we fix our eyes not on what is seen, but on what is unseen. For what is seen is temporary, but what is unseen is eternal. (2 Corinthians 4:16-18)*

That is the perspective of a warrior. The struggles of life are interpreted through different lenses. No longer do you fix your eyes on the Arad attacks on your life that are seen. The warrior in you rises and fixates on what is unseen. The power and presence of a God who is trustworthy. And you follow him in radically obedient steps of faith.

Some of you have left Egypt but keep returning to Hormah. And it may look the same. Same circumstances. Same wounds. Same doubts. But you can look different. You don't have to react the same. You don't have to have the same fear. You don't have to choose what is seen over what is not seen. You can trust God and be who you were made to be.

A warrior.

Leave Egypt once and for all. Take the journey of the exodus. Cross over to the land of promise. It's time to stop walking in circles.

Turn north.

CONCLUSION

Two events have transpired to give Mehran Karimi Nasseri his opportunity for life outside the terminal.

Mehran's lawyer became a warrior on his behalf. After a lengthy legal battle he finally received the necessary documents he needed from the French government that would allow him to reside in France and travel legally.

Curious thing is he refuses to use them. Mehran is convinced he has no official identity. His thinking keeps him enslaved. He believes that if he were to leave France "There are soldiers there who shoot you dead." So he refuses to leave even the first floor of the terminal, much less the airport itself.

"I stay until I obtain my origin identity," he often repeats.[1]

The movie deal is the other event that has provided Mehran an opportunity for a departure. It is reported that Spielberg paid him six figures for the use of his story. He's a wealthy man but continues to live like a wanderer. His address is still the airport. His food is still paid with vouchers. His shower is still the bathroom at night. His bed is still a bench and he still spends his days reading books from a nearby store.[2]

The movie deal may give Mehran a way out, but some doubt he'll ever go. "He has made a place for himself here," said Karima Dubois, who works at the nearby pharmacy that takes his phone calls. "His world is here."[3]

Mehran was not intended to spend his life wandering around an airport. And you were not intended to spend your life wandering around without purpose like a person who cannot be deported.

In the movie version Tom Hank's character, Viktor Navorski, finally does leave the airport. There is something that compels him to take his first cautious steps into his promised land: New York City. That "something" is found in a Planters Peanut can.

Viktor's mission was in the can. His father had attempted to obtain autographs from each jazz player found in a favorite photograph of his. He had acquired all but one before he died and kept them secure in the can. Only one remained to complete the collection. That one last jazz player could be found playing in the lounge of a Ramada Inn in New York City.

It was the mission of his father that caused Viktor to take the steps out of his wilderness into the unknown. And it is the mission of your Father that will compel you to new lands yourself.

He has given you an identity. He has given you the provisions you need. Both are found not in a can but in his Son. Following him will lead you through and out of the wilderness of life.

Along the way there will be struggle and suffering. There will be burning bush moments and faith producing episodes. There will be battles to fight.

But you're ready for them. Your own exodus has prepared you for them. (And maybe this book has helped too.)

You're no longer a wanderer.

You're a warrior.

And your flight is right on schedule.

NOTES

FILE 1: FROM WANDERERS TO WARRIORS

1. Elaine Ganley, "Film May Be Man's Ticket Out of 'Terminal'," August 12, 2004. Found at www.phillyburbs.com/pb-dyn/news/89-08122004-346697.html.

2. We come by that rounded figure by assigning fifty years to a generation and counting Abraham, Isaac, Jacob to Joseph as about 200 years. Then we add the four hundred years of Egyptian captivity mentioned in Acts 7:6.

3. "enormous numbers of tribal groups, most of them Semitic, had been settling in northern Egypt from about 1800 BC. These foreigners had grown so powerful that for a short time they dominated Egypt, ruling the Egyptians themselves..." From *Egypt & the Wanderings*. Found at www.wsu.edu:8080/~dee/HEBREWS/WANDER.HTM.

4. Alexander the Great conquered Egypt in 332 BC.

5. Amhose is not well known but is important to Egyptian history. He is credited with liberating Egypt from the *Habiru* or sometimes called, the "Hyksos." Various scholars attribute different dates to his reign, but he probably became ruler of Egypt around 1550 BC at the age of 10 and ruled for a period of around 25 years before his death. Some are more familiar with the name of his wife, Nefertiri. The Hyksos were an important influence on Egyptian history. Egyptologists sometimes call these people, "asiatics" or "shepherd-kings." Egyptians during the Hyksos invasion designated them as "hikau khausut", which meant "rulers of foreign countries." Today the term Hyksos has come to refer to the whole of these people who ruled Egypt from roughly 1720 to 1550 BC. Mark Healy, *Armies of the Pharaohs* (Osprey Publishing, 1992); Peter A. Clayton, *Chronicle of the Pharaohs: The Reign-By-Reign Record of the Rulers and Dynasties of Ancient Egypt* (Thames and Hudson Ltd; 1994); Ian Shaw and Paul Nicholson, *The Dictionary of Ancient Egypt* (Harry N. Abrams, Inc., 1995).

6. Jano El Kady. Found at www.egyptianchronicles.freewebsitehosting.

7. George Barna, "Morality Continues to Decay," *The Barna Update*, November 3, 2003. Found at barna.org/FlexPage.aspx?Page=BarnaUpdate&BarnaUpdateID=152.

8. George Barna, "Born Again Christians Just as Likely to Divorce as Are Non-Christians," *The Barna Update*, September 8, 2004. Found at www.barna.org/FlexPage.aspx?Page=BarnaUpdate&BarnaUpdateID=170.

9. George Barna, "Number of Unchurched Adults Has Nearly Doubled Since 1991," *The Barna Update*, May 4, 2004. Found at www.barna.org/FlexPage.aspx?Page=BarnaUpdate&BarnaUpdateID=163.

10. George Barna, "Americans Agree: Kids Are Not Being Prepared for Life," *The Barna Update,* October 26, 2004. Found at ww.barna.org/FlexPage.aspx?Page=Barna Update&BarnaUpdateID=173.

11. George Barna, "Spiritual Progress Hard to Find in 2003," *The Barna Update,* December 22, 2003. Found at www.barna.org/FlexPage.aspx?Page=BarnaUpdate& BarnaUpdateID=155.

12. George Barna, "Barna Responds to Christianity Today Article," *The Barna Update,* September 17, 2002. Found at ww.barna.org/FlexPage.aspx?Page=BarnaUpdate& BarnaUpdateID=121.

FILE 2: A TIME FOR WAITING, A TIME FOR WARRING

1. Reggie McNeal, *The Present Future: Six Tough Questions for the Church* (San Francisco: Jossey-Bass, 2003), 3.

2. Jack Dennison, *City Reaching: On the Road to Community Transformation* (Pasadena: William Carey Library, 1999), 116.

3. Ibid, 111.

4. McNeal, *The Present Future,* 4.

5. Elwyn Hartley Edwards, *The Encyclopedia of the Horse* (New York: DK Publishing, Inc., 1994), 111.

FILE 3: I.D.ING WHO YOU ARE

1. Julia Scheeres, "Will It Be Cash, Check or Finger?," October 1, 2001. Found at www.wired.com/news/business/0,1367,47127,00.html.

2. Michael E. Williams, editor, *The Storyteller's Companion to the Bible, Volume Two: Exodus-Joshua* (Nashville: Abingdon Press, 1992), 32.

3. John J. Davis, *Moses and the Gods of Egypt* (Baker Book House: Grand Rapids, 1971), 64.

4. Lance Armstrong Biography, AskMen.com. Found at www.askmen.com/men/ sports/40c_lance_armstrong.html.

FILE 4: FINDING GOD'S MAP FOR YOUR LIFE

1. "Jefferson's Instructions to Meriwether Lewis," Monticello: The Home of Thomas Jefferson website. Found at www.monticello.org/jefferson/Lewisandclark/ instructions.html.

2. Stephen R. Covey, *7 Habits of Highly Effective People* (New York: Simon & Schuster, 1989), 33.

3. Gordon MacDonald, "Building Below the Water Line," October 4, 2004. Found at www.christianitytoday.com/leaders/newsletter/2004/cln41004.html.

FILE 5: IT'S NOT ABOUT YOU!

1. There is a bush that is a variety of the gas plant called the "fraxinella." The plant grows to about three feet in height with clusters of purple blossoms. The whole bush is covered with tiny oil glands. This oil is volatile and a light could make it burst suddenly into flames. See Davis, *Moses and the God's of Egypt*, page 69.

2. See verse 2. Moses thought the bush was on fire. The narrator says that there was a fire from within the bush.

FILE 6: BUCKING THE SYSTEM

1. Tim Dahlberg, "Sportsview: NFL Plays Bad Cop Vs. Plummer," October 15, 2004. Found at www.phillyburbs.com/pb-dyn/news/66-10152004-383133.html.

FILE 7: HOW FAITH CAN BEGIN WITH FEAR

1. Mick Knutson, "Daredevil Jumps from Jesus," December 4, 1999. Found at www.blincmagazine.com/cms/printer_280.shtml.

2. Mick Knutson, "Daredevil Jumps off Rio Christ in Bond-style Stunt," December 3, 1999. Found at www.blincmagazine.com/cms/printer_248.shtml.

FILE 8: EXPECTING RAIN

1. Terence E. Fretheim, *Exodus* (Louisville: John Knox Press, 1991), 182.

FILE 10: MEETING GOD ON THE MOUNTAIN

1. Brian McLaren, "Bless This House? Why efforts to renew the church are often misguided," June 29, 2004. Found at Leadership Journal.net, www.christianity today.com/leaders/newsletter/2004/cln40629.html.

2. Ibid.

FILE 11: THE SPRING OF DECISION

1. See Robert E. Quinn, *Deep Change* (Jossey-Bass: San Francisco, 1996), xii for this concept.

2. Ibid., 24.

FILE 12: HOW TO HANDLE LIFE OVERLOAD.

1. http://www.hyperdictionary.com/dictionary/overload.

2. Compiled from Andrea Hopkins, "Americans Get Plenty of Sleep, Watch Lots of TV," September 15, 2004, found at http://news.myway.com/odd/article/id/427241 oddlyenough|09-15-2004::08:07|reuters.html, and a Denver Post article from Saturday, July 15, 1989 by Andrew Berkowitz of the *San Francisco Chronicle*.

3. Told in John Ortberg, *The Life You've Always Wanted* (Grand Rapids: Zondervan),

90-91.

4. Thanks to Dr. Charles Siburt and Terry Cartwright for these questions.

5. Gary Thomas, *Seeking the Face of God* (Nashville: Thomas Nelson, 1994), 107.

6. Ibid., 103.

FILE 13: DAY PLANNERS, BIG ROCKS, AND PARTIES.

1. Adapted from Stephen Covey, A. Roger Merrill, and Rebecca R. Merrill, *First Things First* (New York: Simon & Schuster, 1994), 88-89.

2. Roland James, "Which Side of the Atlantic is Crazy?" August 29, 2003. Found at www.msnbc.msn.com/id/3072414.

FILE 14: THE TENT STAKE PEOPLE

1. Tibbett L. Speer, "Getting By on Fewer Movers," *American Demographics*, December 1995.

FILE 15: WARRIORS IN THE LAND

1. In scripture this spans from Numbers 14:45-20:1.

2. "Walk by Faith," *Carried Me: The Worship Project*, by Jeremy Camp.

CONCLUSION

1. Ethan Gilsdorf, "Behind 'The Terminal,'" June 21, 2004. Found at www.csmonitor.com/2004/0621/p11s02-almo.html.

2. Behrouz Saba, "'Terminal' Blues: Spielberg Film Misses True Immigrant Story Commentary," June 22, 2004. Found at http://news.pacificnews.org/news/view_article.html?article_id=fbcbc267ea6f23a9da9617647942174b.

3. Elaine Ganley, "Film May Be Man's Ticket Out of 'Terminal'," August 12, 2004. Found at www.phillyburbs.com/pb-dyn/news/89-08122004-346697.html.

ACKNOWLEDGEMENTS

It takes time and effort to shape a book. It takes people to shape a person. Here's thanks to some who have shaped us.

Rick would like to thank:

Lynn Anderson, for stirring a passion for Jesus in the heart of a young college student.

Max Lucado, for helping me see Jesus more clearly, for encouragement to write, and for summer 1980 in Miami. It was a riot.

Tommy King and Terry Cartwright, for letting me learn a love for the Word by watching yours.

The Tomball Church of Christ in Tomball, Texas, for taking a chance on a novice preacher, for your love of Christ (which is amazing), for your love of me (which may be even more amazing) and for listening to these lessons before they were printed.

Jim Herrington, Steve Capper, Nick Senofsky, Galen Blom and Bob Baldwin of Leaders Edge for their steady friendship the past two years.

Stefanni Lynch, for her valuable assistance in proofreading the manuscript.

Bob and Nina Campbell, for giving me Karen.

My parents, Bob and Betty Brown, for their faith and love.

And to my sons, Kristofer and Taylor, for giving up some "Dad" time and encouraging me to write. God must love me because he gave me you.

Reg would like to thank:

Lynn Anderson, for jumping off the preaching notes enough times when I was a college student to present a picture of proclamation that continues to stir my heart.

Friends such as Harold and Jeanette Lipford, Kent Smith, Gailyn Van Rheenen, Gary McCaleb, Bob Strader, Jan Meyer, Brad Small, and countless others at Abilene

Christian who put up with, believed in, and supported me as God refined my character, gifts, and passion. I'm nothing but the fruit of your love.

Fun Hog's such as Kevin Roberts, Glen Villanueva, Bella and Jerry Maldonado, Richmond Frasier, Terry Cox, and many other tent mates, riding partners, rock addicts, altitude junkies, and lovers of the wide open for stepping out there with me to see just how far we could push the envelope in the name of adventure and friendship.

The Lakewood Church of Christ family, especially the amazing staff and elders who believe in me and are crazy enough to cut loose the ropes of convention so we can soar towards the Spirit's ideal together.

My mom, my late Grandmother Zona, the Cox, Thornton, Sanderson, and William's families for loving someone as impetuous and full of loud dreams as me.

And my son Levi and daughter Faith Ann...there just isn't words to describe how cool it is to be your dad.

Finally, we'd both like to thank Leonard Allen for his keen editorial eye, his spiritual guidance, his brotherly encouragement, and for giving us this opportunity. Thank you for pursuing excellence, truth, faith, and God's heart in every aspect of your personal and professional life. We'd pack up and head out into the wilderness in search of the promises of God with you any day.

Reg Cox & Rick Brown